# SOURCES, STORIES, AND SONGS

## ANTHOLOGY

# Regions

## ADVENTURES IN TIME AND PLACE

- **Advertisements**
- **Biographies and Autobiographies**
- **Diaries**
- **Fiction and Nonfiction Selections**
- **Folk Tales and Fables**
- **Letters**
- **Plays**
- **Poems**
- **Songs**
- **Speeches and Interviews**
- **Visual Documents**

McGraw-Hill
School Division

New York     Farmington

## PROGRAM AUTHORS

**Dr. James A. Banks**
Professor of Education and Director of the Center for Multicultural Education
University of Washington
Seattle, Washington

**Dr. Barry K. Beyer**
Professor Emeritus, Graduate School of Education
George Mason University
Fairfax, Virginia

**Dr. Gloria Contreras**
Professor of Education
University of North Texas
Denton, Texas

**Jean Craven**
District Coordinator of Curriculum Development
Albuquerque Public Schools
Albuquerque, New Mexico

**Dr. Gloria Ladson-Billings**
Professor of Education
University of Wisconsin
Madison, Wisconsin

**Dr. Mary A. McFarland**
Instructional Coordinator of Social Studies, K–12, and Director of Staff Development
Parkway School District
Chesterfield, Missouri

**Dr. Walter C. Parker**
Professor and Program Chair for Social Studies Education
University of Washington
Seattle, Washington

NATIONAL GEOGRAPHIC SOCIETY
Washington, D.C.

## Acknowledgments

"The Heavy Pants of Mr. Strauss" from THE SPICE OF AMERICA by June Swanson. Text copyright ©1983 by June Swanson. Published by Carolrhoda Books, Inc., Minneapolis, MN.

"The Buffalo Go" from AMERICAN INDIAN MYTHOLOGY by Alice Marriott and Carol K. Rachlin. ©1968 by Alice Marriott and Carol K. Rachlin. HarpersCollins Publishers.

HEARTLAND by Diane Siebert. Text ©1989 by Diane Siebert. Illustration ©1989 by Wendell Minor. HarperCollins Publishers.

SIERRA by Diane Siebert. Text ©1991 by Diane Siebert. Illustration ©1991 by Wendell Minor. HarperCollins Publishers.

Excerpt from HECTOR LIVES IN THE UNITED STATES NOW by Joan Hewett. ©1990 by Joan Hewett. HarperCollins Publishers.

"I Pledge a Lesson to the Frog" from IN THE YEAR OF THE BOAR AND JACKIE ROBINSON by Bette Bao Lord. ©1984 by Bette Bao Lord. HarperCollins Publishers.

*(continued on page 174)*

*McGraw-Hill School Division*
*A Division of The McGraw·Hill Companies*

McGraw-Hill School Division
Two Penn Plaza
New York, New York 10121

Printed in the United States of America

ISBN 0-02-147599-7 / 4

6 7 8 9 079 02 01

# TABLE OF *Contents*

# USING PRIMARY SOURCES AND LITERATURE WITH SOCIAL STUDIES

The readings in the *Adventures in Time and Place Anthology* have been carefully selected to enhance social studies concepts and to provide enjoyable and worthwhile reading experiences for students. All readers bring to the reading experience their own backgrounds and prior knowledge. Exposing students to a variety of viewpoints while encouraging them to question and ponder what they read will help them to become critical readers and thoughtful citizens.

The readings include **primary sources, secondary sources,** and **literature.** These fall into several categories, including:

- songs
- official documents
- oral histories
- posters
- diaries and journals
- photographs and graphics
- personal recollections
- poems
- folk tales
- letters
- autobiographies and biographies
- newspaper articles
- fiction and nonfiction
- speeches

The readings offer you a unique teaching tool. The following suggestions will help your students use the readings to build and extend their knowledge of social studies as well as to sharpen their analytical skills.

## PRIMARY AND SECONDARY SOURCES

A **primary source** is something that comes from the time that is being studied. Primary sources include such things as official documents of the time, diaries and journals, letters, newspaper articles and advertisements, photographs, and oral histories. A **secondary source** is an account of the past written by someone who was not an eyewitness to those events. Remind students of the difference between primary and secondary sources. Point out that primary sources give historians valuable clues from the past because they provide firsthand information about a certain time or event. Primary sources let the reader see how people lived, felt, and thought.

However, primary sources express the view of only one person. Thus, it is important for students to understand the point of view of the writer and to find out all that they can about his or her background to decide whether the writer is credible, or believable. Secondary sources often compare and analyze different points of view and give a broader view of the event. Once again, however, it is important for students to understand the writer's point of view and analyze his or her credentials.

Suggest to students that, when they read primary and secondary sources, they ask themselves these questions:

- Who created the source?
- Can the writer be believed?
- Does the writer have expert knowledge of the subject?
- Does the writer have a reason to describe the events in a certain way?
- Does the writer have a reputation for being accurate?

You may wish to encourage students to think about the following as they read some of the various sources:

**Autobiographies** What role did the subject of the autobiography play in history? Did the person live during a critical time in history? How was the person influenced by the time in which he or she lived?

**Diaries and Journals** Was the diary or journal originally written to be shared with the public? Was it commissioned by a government official, such as the Columbus log was?

**Speeches** Was the intent of the speech to persuade the audience to adopt a particular point of view or was the speech merely informative?

**Interviews** Who is the person being interviewed? What is his or her point of view?

**Advertisements** What is the purpose of the advertisement? Does it make any statements about the product that seem questionable? If so, how could you check them out?

## LITERATURE

In social studies, literature is used to motivate and instruct. It also plays a large role in assisting students to understand their cultural heritage and the cultural heritage of others. For example, the folk tales included in the *Adventures in Time and Place Anthology*, such as "The Buffalo Go" from the Kiowa culture, were chosen to offer students glimpses of the wisdom various cultures deem important to impart. The songs, stories, and poetry of different cultures offer students opportunities to compare and contrast and hence understand aspects of cultural identity. Nonfiction selections, such as *50 Simple Things Kids Can Do to Save the Earth*, give students opportunities to read informational text that applies to current and historical real-life issues.

**I**n *Regions* you will be reading about many different people, places, and times. This Anthology, or collection of documents created by different people, will make the information in your textbook come to life in a special way. The Anthology includes stories, songs, poems, diaries, interviews, letters, plays, and old advertisements and posters. As you read and study these documents, you will be able to see, feel, and hear what it is like to live in other places. Your Anthology will even take you back into the past and help you feel what it was like to live in other times! The selections in your Anthology will help you to better understand life in diverse regions of the United States, both past and present.

**CASSETTE LOGO •**
Tells you that the selection appears on the Anthology Cassette

**TEXTBOOK LINK •**
Tells you which chapter and lesson in your textbook the document is linked to

**CONCLUSION •**
Provides additional information and asks you to think further about the selection

**INTRODUCTION •**
Gives you background information about the selection and tells you what kind of document it is. Is it fiction or nonfiction? Is it a poem or a song? The introduction also asks you a question to think about as you read the document.

**DEFINITIONS •**
Gives you the meanings of difficult words

**SOURCE •**
Tells you where the selection came from

---

Use with Chapter 3, Lesson 1

## THE NEW COLOSSUS

by Emma Lazarus, 1883

When France gave the United States the Statue of Liberty as a gift in 1880, Emma Lazarus was moved to write the poem, The New Colossus. A colossus is something gigantic. Emma Lazarus was born in New York City in 1849. As a young woman, she saw both her city and the United States change with the constant flow of immigrants from other countries. Many arrived penniless, carrying just a bundle of clothing. But they also came with great dreams of starting a new life in a new land. Who is the Statue of Liberty welcoming?

Not like the brazen giant of Greek fame,
With conquering limbs astride from land to land;
Here at our sea-washed, sunset gates shall stand
A mighty woman with a torch, whose flame
Is the imprisoned lightning, and her name
Mother of Exiles. From her beacon-hand
Glows world-wide welcome; her mild eyes command
The air-bridged harbor that twin cities frame.

"Keep, ancient lands, your storied pomp!" cries she
With silent lips. "Give me your tired, your poor,
Your huddled masses yearning to breathe free,
The wretched refuse of your teeming shore.
Send these, the homeless, tempest-tost to me,
I lift my lamp beside the golden door!"

brazen: bold
conquering: mighty
astride: with one leg on each side

imprisoned: captured
exiles: people forced out of their countries
beacon-hand: hand that holds a guiding light
storied pomp: old habits and fancy ways
huddled masses: crowds of poor people
wretched refuse: unwanted people
teeming: crowded
tempest-tost: battered by storms

The New Colossus was carved into a bronze plaque and mounted at the base of the Statue of Liberty when the statue was completed in 1886. Today, the statue still welcomes people coming to the United States through New York Harbor. The statue symbolizes hope and freedom to millions of people throughout the world.

Source: Emma Lazarus, Poems of Emma Lazarus. Boston: Houghton-Mifflin Company, 1889.

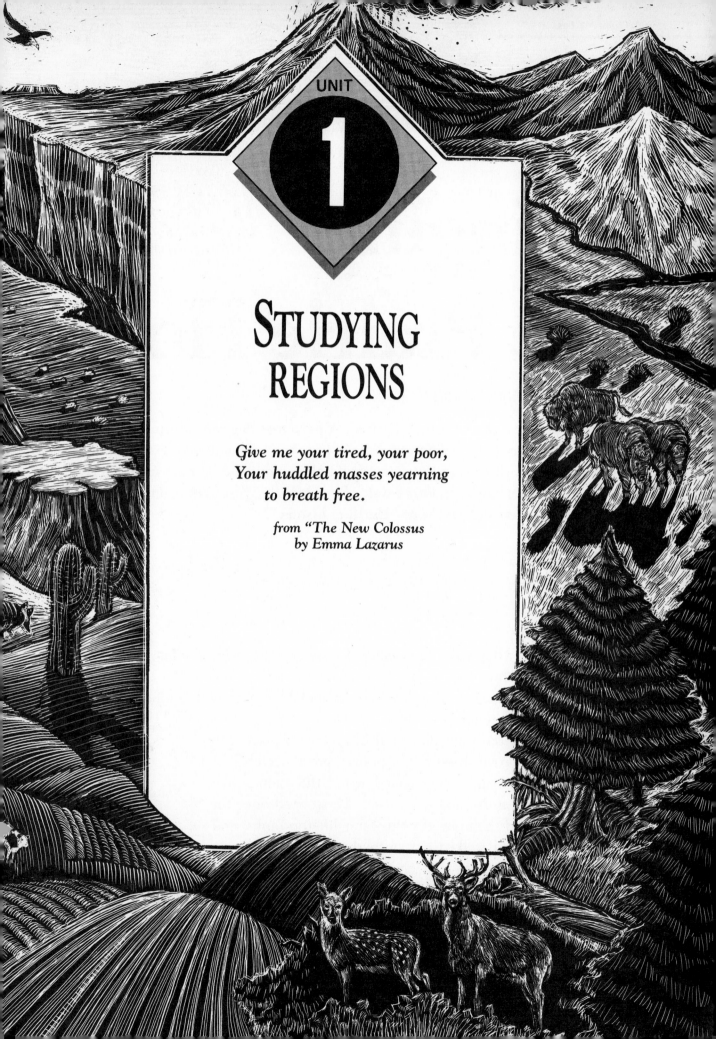

# STUDYING REGIONS

*Give me your tired, your poor,
Your huddled masses yearning
to breath free.*

*from "The New Colossus
by Emma Lazarus*

# Bringing the Prairie Home

**by Patricia MacLachlan**

*Where we live influences how we live. A person who grows up in the Rocky
Mountains may have a different view of life than someone who grows up in
a busy city. In this essay Patricia MacLachlan says she became who she is
because of the prairie, or grassland, of the Middle West. What do you think
she means when she says that "Earth is history"?*

Place.

This is one of my favorite words and I am a writer
because of it.

Place.

I remember **vividly** the place where I was born: the smell
of the earth, the look of the skies when storms came
through; the softness of my mother's **hollyhock** blooms that
grew by the back fence.

When I was ten years old, I fell in love with place. My
parents and I drove through the prairie, great stretches of
land between small towns named wonderful names like
Spotted Horse, Rattlesnake, Sunrise. We stopped once for
drinks that we fished out of cold-water lift-top tanks, and
my mother and I walked out onto the prairie. Then my
mother said something that changed my life forever. She
took a step, looked down at her footprint, and said, "Someone long ago may have walked here, or maybe no one ever
has. Either way it's history."

**vividly:** clearly

**hollyhock:** tall plant
with large, showy
flowers

2

I thought of those who might have come before me and those who might come after, but mostly I was face-to-face with the important, hopeful **permanence** of place, place that I knew was there long before I walked there, and would be there long after I was gone. I realized, in that moment, that the Earth is history. The Earth is like a character who has secrets; the Earth holds important clues to who we are, who we've been; who we will be. We are connected to the land and to those secrets.

It was after this event that I bought a diary and began writing all sorts of truths about myself, as if I, too, might leave clues about myself behind. I was becoming a writer. All because of place. Now I cannot write a story unless I know the place, the **landscape** that shapes the story and the people in the story. And to remind myself of the place that changed me, I have carried a small bag of prairie dirt with me for years.

I took that bag of prairie dirt with me once to a class of fourth graders, and I found that those children are connected to place, too. Some had moved from place to place many times: One boy's house had burned in a fire recently; another was about to move to a place he had never been.

"Maybe," I said, "I should toss this out onto my New England yard. I'll probably never live on the prairie again."

"*No!*" cried a boy, horrified. "It might blow away!"

And then a girl had a suggestion.

"Maybe you should put that prairie dirt in a glass on your windowsill, so you can see it when you write. It would be like bringing the prairie home."

And that is where that little piece of my prairie is today; my place, my past, my landscape; in a glass on my windowsill. I have brought the prairie home so that I can look at it every day; write about it, write about me, and remind myself that the land is the connection that links us all.

**permanence:** state of lasting forever

**landscape:** stretch of scenery

*MacLachlan brought a bag of prairie dirt to her new home to remind her of the land where she was born. If you were to save something to remind you of the place where you live, what object would you choose? Why?*

Source: Patricia MacLachlan, "Bringing the Prairie Home," *The Big Book of Planet Earth*. New York: Dutton Children's Books, 1993.

3

# STATES AND CAPITALS

## by Professor Rap

*As you know, our country is made up of 50 states. Each of these states has something special about it, and each state has a capital city where the state's government is located. Have you ever tried to memorize all of the states and their capitals? It's not an easy job. Professor Rap is a singer whose rap songs make learning social studies fun. How does Professor Rap use rhymes to teach the states and their capitals in the rap song below?*

You got to learn, and get an education
Learn the states and capitals of our nation
We'll help you learn, border-to-border
So we'll start in alphabetical order
Alabama . . . in the south and summery
Its capital rhymes . . . Montgomery
In Alaska, there's always snow
Capital city . . . Juneau
It's easy to learn if you associate a rhyme
So let's keep it going, you're doing fine
It's pretty easy . . . pretty good
You kind of like it? . . . I knew you would

Arizona's is Phoenix . . . home of the cactus
This you will learn . . . with some practice
Little Rock's the capital of Arkansas
Now did you see who we just saw. . .
In California (Totally!) at the state's capital
Sacramento (Dude!) pretty radical
Colorado's capital is Denver
Heard the mountains are nice, but
   never been there
It's pretty easy . . . pretty good
You kind of like it? . . . I knew you would

Hartford's the capital . . . of Connecticut
Sit up straight . . . it's proper etiquette
Delaware's capital . . . is Dover
Red Rover, Red Rover, send Billy right over
Florida, capital . . . Tallahassee
Lots of oranges, vitamin C
Atlanta is the capital of Georgia
Pay attention . . . we won't bore ya
Hawaii, capital . . . Honolulu
Tropical paradise, ocean blue
(ocean blue) . . . pretty good
You kind of like it? . . . I knew you would
It's pretty easy . . . pretty good
Boise's the capital of Idaho
Farmer Jack, getting busy growing . . .
   potatoes
Springfield's the capital of Illinois
Get up everybody, let's make some noise
In Indiana, cars go real fast
In the capital city of Indianapolis
Iowa's capital . . . is Des Moines
If you're not rappin' now, would you
   care to join?

Topeka . . . capital of Kansas
Walkin' the yellow brick road, you'll
   take some chances
It's pretty easy . . . pretty good
You kind of like it? . . . I knew you would
Frankfort's the capital of Kentucky
Finger lickin' good, let's get funky
Louisiana's capital is Baton Rouge
Hard to miss, the state is shaped like a boot
Augusta is the capital of Maine
And its lobsters are their claim-to-fame
Annapolis . . . the capital of Maryland
At the Naval Academy . . . boys
   become men
It's pretty easy . . . pretty good
You kind of like it? . . . I knew you would
Massachusetts' is Boston . . . raised the
   tax on the tea
The people didn't like it, threw it in the sea
Michigan's capital . . . is Lansing
Woods and lakes . . . hunting and fishing
Minnesota, capital . . . St. Paul
All for one, and one for all

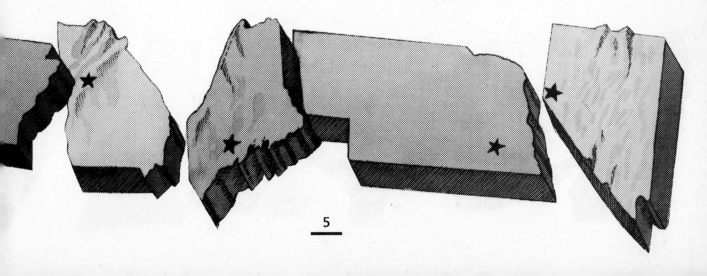

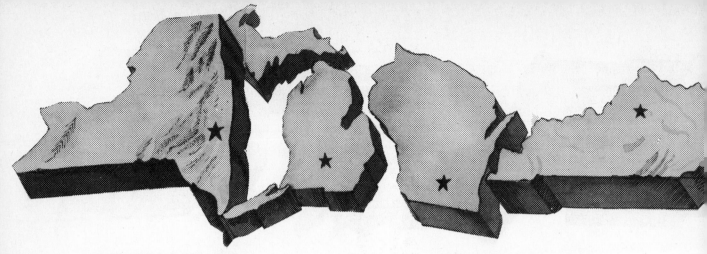

M-I-S-S-I-S-S-I-P-P-I
Jackson, Mississippi, where rivers run wide
Jefferson City, the capital of Missouri
Half way there . . . no need to worry
(Break down): G-G-G-Get down
Professor Rap's rocking the mike to a
    new sound
(Repeat and add groove)
The Continental Divide is in Montana
And the capital city is Helena
Nebraska is the Cornhusker State
Lincoln is the capital, keep up the pace
Nevada, capital . . . Carson City
Not learning your capitals would be a pity
New Hampshire, capital . . . Concord
Keep singing this rhyme 'cause you're
    not getting bored
Trenton is the capital . . . of New Jersey
A beautiful state set beside the sea
New Mexico . . . an enchanting place
And its capital city is Santa Fe
It's pretty easy . . . pretty good
You kind of like it? . . . I knew you would

New York . . . America's "Melting Pot"
Albany's its capital in case you forgot
North Carolina's capital is Raleigh
If you do good, you may get a lolly "POP!"
Bismarck's the capital of North Dakota
Home to the Sioux, and did you
    know that. . .
The Buckeye State is Ohio
The capital's Columbus, so let's go. . .
To Oklahoma . . . a-do-wah-ditty
Capital's simple . . . Oklahoma City
It's pretty easy . . . pretty good
You kind of like it? . . . I knew you would
Oregon's capital . . . is Salem
Guess what? (WHAT?) we're almost done
Pennsylvania . . . producer of steel
Harrisburg's the capital, these facts are
    for real
It's pretty easy . . . pretty good
You kind of like it? . . . I knew you would
Rhode Island's capital is Providence,
    it's evident
One of the 13 colonies to achieve
    independence

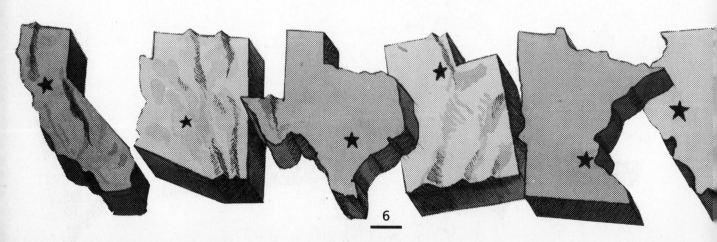

Let's go . . . to South Carolina
We'll visit the capital, Columbia
South Dakota has clean crisp air
And its capital city is Pierre
Nashville's the capital of Tennessee
Let's all go to the Jamboree
(Country break)
Austin's the capital of Texas (WHOO!)
Hold on tight when you're riding that
    bronco
Salt Lake City is what we'll call
The capital city of Utah
Montpelier is the capital of Vermont
And you can rap along with us if you want
Virginia was the home to George
    Washington
And its capital city is Richmond
It's pretty easy . . . pretty good
You kind of like it? . . . I knew you would
Olympia's the capital of Washington
Three more (Yeah?) we're almost done
West Virginia, capital . . . Charleston
Learning like this can be a lot of fun

Wisconsin . . . the Dairy State
Madison's the capital . . . can you relate
Wyoming's capital is Cheyenne
You did it . . . now give yourself a hand
    (YAA!)
It's pretty easy . . . pretty good
You kind of like it? . . . I knew you would
Now you've learned the states and
    capitals of our nation
But, there's one more capital that we
    should mention
I bet you've guessed it, because it's so easy
The District of Columbia, or
    Washington, D.C.
It's our nation's capital, where all the
    laws are made
And home of the President of the U.S.A.
Well, have fun learning, and remember
    the rules. . .
Say "NO" to drugs . . . and stay in school
It's pretty easy . . . pretty good
You kind of like it? . . . I knew you would

Source: Rick Kott, "States & Capitals." Utica, MI: Dalka Studios, 1990.

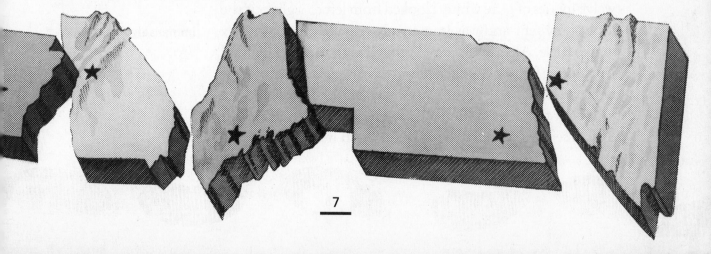

# A Walk Across America

### by Peter Jenkins

*On October 15, 1973, a young man named Peter Jenkins
from Alfred, New York, went out for a walk—across the entire
United States! With his faithful dog, Cooper, Jenkins spent six
years walking across the country. He hiked over mountains
and across plains and deserts. In 1984 Jenkins wrote a book
about his adventures. In the following passage he describes
hiking up the Appalachians in Virginia. What season does Jenkins
describe here? How does climate affect this part of his journey?*

My eyes opened to a country blue sky that met with
twelve inches of pure white. I looked from left to right out the
front of my tent and was **immensely** relieved that I wasn't a
human icicle. Alive and warm, I wanted to stay in my beautiful
sleeping bag forever. Cooper, however, clawed at the tent floor
to tell me he wanted out into his dream world. I unzipped the
front door to our home and out he jumped. He was as excited
as a kid seeing Santa for the first time, and he had to share it

**immensely:** greatly

with someone. Of course, that unlucky person was me. After a few minutes of bounding through the **pristine** powder, he crashed into the tent covered with snow and lovingly rolled over on me.

Seeing that he was making me fighting mad, he then licked my face with his bad morning breath, strong enough to **singe** my red beard. I tried desperately to crawl deeper into the bag and escape his snowy joy. Too excited to notice, he left the tent. I closed my eyes to get a little more sleep. No sooner had I relaxed when coo-coo Cooper got the cord that held up the front of the tent in his mouth and yanked the tent down with a mighty pull.

Red with rage, I shot out of the sleeping bag far enough to reach outside from under the fallen door into the snow. With both strong hands, I molded a snowball as hard as I could and when teasing Cooper came back to the front, I threw it hard, hoping to hit him in the head. Oh! I was mad! To him that snowball was more fun than baseball so from that day on, Cooper started our winter wake-up, warm-up tradition.

Inching my way far enough out of the cocoonlike bag, I sat up and put on my fluffy down jacket. Then I reached down in the bottom of the six-foot-long sleeping bag and pulled out a variety of crumpled clothes that I left there through the night to keep them warm. My **wadded-up** pants went on, ever so carefully, making sure my body wasn't out of the cozy bag before the warm pants covered the bare spots. With my body all covered, I painfully crawled out of the motherly sleeping blanket and rammed my perfume-producing white socks over my chilly feet. The only thing left to do before we could hit the road was to put on my frosted new boots. The sweat from the day before had **condensed** on the inside of the boots and turned to ice. First my right foot was frozen awake and then my left; it was a battle between the **frigid** frost and the warmth of my feet. My feet won and the stiffened boots stayed on for another traveling day. With that done, I then edged out into the world.

Instead of a steaming cup of coffee, my wake-up **tonic** was taking down the tent. This morning the back end of the tent sagged with six inches of new snow. The front end had already come down with Cooper's pranks, so taking off the rain fly was harder than usual. As I bent slowly to untie the cords from the tent stakes, I heard a fluffy charge from behind. Before I could

turn around, Cooper, the muscle-bound elf, was in the air. The next time I saw him he was on top of me. Both of us flattened the once sturdy tent, and there I lay crunched. He was so excited he barked in **hyper** screams. On the rebound, he was off again, darting through the snow as beautifully as a swimming seal.

Again, I reached down into the deep snow and made another snowball. This time I threw it as hard as a pitcher in the World Series and bouncing Cooper caught it in his mouth. Then he trotted over to me and dropped the shattered pieces of the snowball into my hand and ran back into the white field. At about fifty feet he turned around, wagged his tail and barked the way he always did when we used to play throw-the-stick. Shaking my head, I melted. I just couldn't stay mad at this happy dog who only wanted to play. My **irresistible** friend brought, for the thousandth time, a smile like all the sunshine to my face. We played throw-the-snowball-and-run for at least an hour.

The sun was high overhead by the time everything was packed up and ready to go. Back on the road, all I wanted to do was get to North Carolina. It looked only four or five days away, and North Carolina sounded much warmer than West Virginia or Virginia. What slowed us down more than I had expected was all the **continuously** curving roads. On the maps, they looked so straight. Another thing that the maps never told me was that these roads often decided to go up a mountain for four, five, or ten miles at a time. Only a few curves would give some kind of slight relief. For two days crossing through the Jefferson National Forest, we wound our way up and down and up and down through the blowing snow. The farther we went, the more **desolate** and lonely it became. People and stores were almost **extinct**, and it really got bad when we took a left on Highway 16 past Tazewell, Virginia.

We walked over mountains as high as 4,705 feet [1,434 m], weakened by lack of food. It seemed that in this draining cold I could never get enough to eat, even if there had been a store every five miles. We were lucky if we came upon one every fifteen. Then came the mountain that almost made me give up.

We camped early because that mountain stood before us and I knew that this late in the day I shouldn't even try it. I hiked through some bare fields to the top of a wooded hill, set

**hyper:** excited

**irresistible:** charming

**continuously:** without stopping

**desolate:** empty
**extinct:** disappeared

up the tent, crawled in, and fell asleep. Cooper was in no mood for play, and he too went to sleep before it was dark.

The morning dawned much too early and we arose in slow motion. Even happy Cooper seemed **lethargic**. He moved at a stumble, like a black bear just waking up from **hibernation**. The whole day was darkened by the gray-black storm clouds blowing in from the west. I took the frosted tent down and we walked down a stubby, cut-over field to the road. There were no houses or stores in sight, so we walked as our shrinking stomachs started burning what little fat we had for fuel. Before us were miles of "Man-eater Mountain." Stubbornly, we started up and went up, and up, and up. Every mile or two I would slow down to a snail's pace because slowing down was the only way I could rest. If I sat down in the warmth-sucking snow, I was afraid I might fall sleep.

I fought **depression**. Our enemy became the mountain, and Route 16 became the way to win. Finally I could see it! One mountaintop higher than all the rest and maybe, just maybe, that was the top of Man-eater Mountain. My damp, wrinkled map told me that if I could struggle to the top, I would be able to coast down to the town of Chattam Hill, Virginia, population 58, and please, . . . an **oasis**? I hadn't seen anything human for at least fifteen desolate miles.

I pushed and pushed my aching self and called forth all of my **waning** stores of energy. One hundred feet from me and three hundred from Cooper was the top of Man-eater Mountain. We made it! **Hysterically** I called Cooper.

Screaming, "Cooper! There's the top!" Something in the tone of my holler made Coops run and a few sprinting minutes later we were there. It didn't matter that "there" was in the middle of nowhere: we had made it to the top.

**lethargic:** sleepy

**hibernation:** a long winter sleep

**depression:** sadness

**oasis:** safe resting spot

**waning:** lessening

**hysterically:** with a lot of emotion

*Jenkins made it across the Appalachians. He also made it across the Great Plains and over the Rocky Mountains, finally reaching the Pacific Ocean in 1979—six years after he first set off. In his remarkable journey, Jenkins walked almost 5,000 miles (8,045 km).*

Source: Peter Jenkins, *A Walk Across America*. Carmel, NY: Guidepost Publishing Company, 1979.

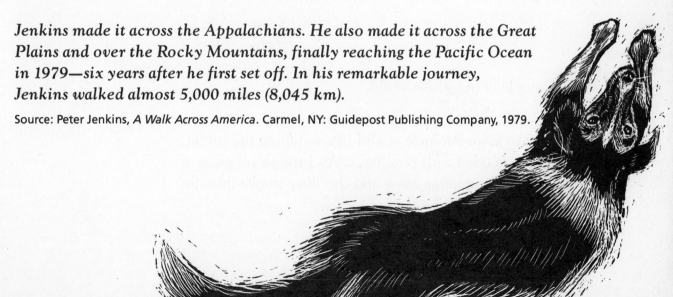

# Dear World

**edited by Lannis Temple**

*Children all over the world are concerned about their country's resources and environment. Lannis Temple traveled around the world to ask children about their thoughts, hopes, and fears concerning the environment. Here are a few of the letters Temple collected. What do the writers enjoy in nature? What do they wish would change?*

To everyone,

    I wish I could be an interpreter and translate the words of animals to my friends and teachers. I saw people throwing things into the river and also throwing all their **rubbish** left by the side of the river and I think if grown-ups do such things then children will imitate them and throw bits of cakes and sweets into the river and on to the side of the road. In the river we could swim in the past but as a dam was constructed, water in the river became dirty.

    If the oceans and rivers could talk, I'd like to hear what they had to say about man. If I could hear them this is what I think they would have said. 'We had clear water in the past but as time went by dams and factories were built and our previously clean water became dirty. We want human beings to be concerned more honestly about the seas and rivers.'

*Sanae Kuwana, Age 11*
Japan—Shikoku

**rubbish:** garbage

Dear people of the whole world,
    take care of nature.

    I like to swim but most of all I like watching the sunset. The sky is flooded with pink light. And the factories, as if out of spite, are puffing away and the dirty smoke drifts in the pink sky. And I want to shout for all the world to hear: 'Do not pollute the air.' I nearly cry. And at night when it's dark and the factories are quiet I look at the stars. I am filled with freedom and happiness. And at that moment only my cat understands me. We sit and gaze at the beautiful sky.

Your friend, a friend of nature:
*Natasha Manayenkova, Age 10*
Russia—Siberia

Hi, Dear friends,

Last night I dreamed the whole world had changed. All these dry lands had been turned into a beautiful nature full of trees, full of rivers, and the sky had become blue. War and bloodshed had ended. All the countries around the world were united, and they lived peacefully together.

I found in my dream all these trees, parks were full of trees and flowers, and kids joyfully were playing around there, and also the beautiful sun was talking to the people. Everybody was happy. Jungles were full of animals. All those animals were also happy. Nobody was sick or ill. All the trees in the streets were green. Nobody was using any car which was giving off smoke. Instead all those machines were using the energy of the sun. Suddenly, when I woke up, I found out it was a dream. But I wish the world would be like my dream.

Yours faithfully,
*Hamidreza Modaberi, Age 11*
Iran

*If you were to write back to one of these children, what would you tell him or her about our country's environment? How do you think children around the world can help to use natural resources wisely?*

Source: Lannis Temple, ed., *Dear World: How Children Around the World Feel About Our Environment*. New York: Random House, 1993.

# 50 Simple Things Kids Can Do To Save the Earth

### by John Javna and the EarthWorks Group

*Children and adults realize that everyone has to help to protect the environment if we want to enjoy our natural resources in the future. What you may not realize is that you can make a difference! An organization called the EarthWorks Group has printed a book called 50 Simple Things Kids Can Do to Save the Earth. Here are a few of their suggestions. Which ones might you like to try?*

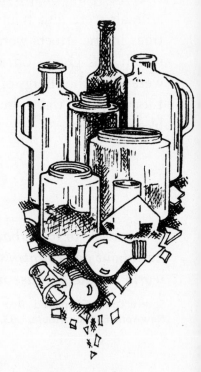

### BE A BOTTLE BANDIT
### Take a Guess
#### *What is glass made from?*
**A) Frozen water      B) Sand      C) Venetian blinds**

**L**ight bulbs, windows, TVs, mirrors...What do they all have in common? Glass.

Look around. See how much glass we use. Now here's an amazing thought: We throw most of our glass away.

Every month, we toss out enough glass bottles and jars to fill up a giant skyscraper.

You probably think this doesn't make much sense, since we're just making more garbage and wasting the Earth's treasures besides. And you're right.

This is especially true because we can reuse them!

### Did You Know?

• Glass is **recycled** at factories where they break bottles and jars into little bits, then melt them down and mix them with new glass.

**recycled:** used again

**Answer: B.** That's right, glass is made from heating and molding sand.

- People have been making glass for over 3,000 years. So when **Nero** was fiddling in ancient Rome, he probably had a bottle of something to drink right next to him.

  **Nero:** an emperor of ancient Rome

- For a long time, glass was considered **precious.** Then people got so good at making it that we started thinking of it as garbage.

  **precious:** very valuable

- Now we throw out 28 billion bottles and jars every year!
- Recycling glass saves energy for making new glass. The energy saved from recycling one glass bottle will light a 100-watt light bulb for four hours.

## *What You Can Do*

**To recycle glass bottles and jars in your home:**
- Find a place you can keep a box or two for collecting glass.
- If you have enough room, keep a different box for each different color of glass—brown, green, clear. Otherwise, you might have to sort the glass later.
- Take the caps, corks or rings off the bottles and jars. It's okay to leave the paper labels on, but rinse the glass out before you put it in the box.
- Once you've got a place to put the glass, it only takes about 15 minutes a week to keep up the recycling.
- Ask an adult to find out where the nearest recycling center is. Your neighborhood may even have curbside recycling.

## *STAMP OUT STYROFOAM*
### *Take a Guess*
*If you lined up all the styrofoam cups made in just one day, how far would they reach?*
**A) 1 mile     B) Around the earth     C) Across the U.S.**

**Y**ou may not know the word "Styrofoam," but you know the stuff. It's a kind of material we use for things like throwaway cups, packing things in boxes, and for keeping "food to go" warm. Lots of fast-food restaurants serve their hamburgers in Styrofoam packages.

Styrofoam is a kind of plastic, so making it uses up treasures that have been on the Earth for billions of years.

**Answer: B. Incredible! They would circle the entire planet . . . and reach a little further, too!**

And what do we do with it? Go take a look in a fast-food garbage can. Does that **styro-trash** look like the Earth's treasures to you? Not anymore!

Using Styrofoam means using up precious resources... and adding more garbage to our world. Is that what you want? Or do you—and your planet—deserve something better?

**styro-trash:** discarded Styrofoam

### Did You Know?

- Styrofoam is permanent garbage. It can't ever become part of the earth again. Five hundred years from now a [child] might be digging in his [or her] backyard and find a piece of the Styrofoam cup you drank lemonade from on a picnic last week!

- Styrofoam is a danger to sea animals. Floating in the water, it looks like their food. But when they eat it, they're in trouble. Sea turtles, for example, sometimes eat Styrofoam and then—because it makes them float—can't dive again. It eventually clogs their systems, and then they starve to death.

### What You Can Do

- Avoid Styrofoam. Such plastic foam is often made with chemicals that make the **ozone** hole bigger!

- If you eat at fast-food restaurants, ask for paper cups and plates. If the people at the restaurant say they don't have them, explain why you don't want to use Styrofoam. Tell them that, as much as you like their food, you really don't want to do anything to hurt the Earth.

- Try to avoid Styrofoam products like picnic plates, cups, and even (if you ever go food shopping) egg cartons.

**ozone:** a layer of air high above Earth that protects the planet from harmful rays from the sun

## SHOWER POWER
### Take a Guess
*How many half-gallon milk cartons can you fill with the water from a five-minute shower?*
A) 5    B) 15    C) 50

**Answer: C.** Think how high 50 milk cartons stacked on top of one another would reach.

**W**hat if you turned on the faucet and no water came out? We need to save water now so that will never happen!

### Did You Know?

- When you shower, you use five gallons of water every minute! How much is that? Enough to fill 40 big glasses!
- A whole shower usually takes at least five minutes. So every day, you could use 25 gallons of water taking one shower.
- In a year, that's almost 10,000 gallons for your showers!
- Taking a bath uses even more water than showers—about twice as much. A bath can easily use 50 gallons of water.
- Shower Secret: People can put in a special "low-flow" shower head. This adds air to the water, so it cuts the amount of shower water used from five gallons a minute to two-and-a-half. That's half as much water! But it feels great!

### What You Can Do

- Take showers instead of baths. This saves water right away. One bonus: singing in a shower sounds better than in a bath.
- Tell your parents about "low-flow" shower heads. Believe it or not, most grown-ups have never heard of them. You could even phone the hardware store to help find one. Or write a letter to Ecological Water Products, 1341 West Main Rd., Middletown, RI 02840 and ask for information. (If you do this, don't forget to show it to your parents.)

*More and more students are getting involved in the fight to clean up pollution and save energy. In the early 1990s many students decided not to buy food packaged in Styrofoam. Now many fast-food restaurants have stopped using Styrofoam products completely! What other ways can you think of to help protect our environment?*

**Source:** John Javna and the EarthWorks Group, *50 Simple Things Kids Can Do to Save the Earth.* Kansas City: Andrews and McMeel, 1990.

# I Hear America Singing

**by Walt Whitman, 1856**

*Walt Whitman was a schoolteacher, a nurse in the Civil War, a newspaper reporter, a clerk for the United States government, and also a famous American poet! Whitman's poems celebrated the "common man" in America—regular people like workers and parents and immigrants. Who are the Americans he hears singing in "I Hear America Singing"?*

I hear America singing, the varied carols I hear,
Those of mechanics, each one singing his as it should be
    **blithe** and strong,

> **blithe:** happy

The carpenter singing his as he measures his plank or
    beam,
The **mason** singing his as he makes ready for work, or
    leaves off work,

> **mason:** someone who builds with stone

The boatman singing what belongs to him in his boat, the
    deck-hand singing on the steamboat deck.
The shoemaker singing as he sits on his bench, the hatter
    singing as he stands,
The wood-cutter's song, the **ploughboy**'s on his way in the
    morning or at noon intermission or at sundown,

> **ploughboy:** boy who plows fields on a farm

The delicious singing of the mother, or of the young wife
    at work, or of the girl sewing or washing,
Each singing what belongs to him or her and to none else,
The day what belongs to the day—at night the party of
    young fellows, **robust**, friendly,

> **robust:** strong, healthy

Singing with open mouths their strong **melodious** songs.

> **melodious:** tuneful

*Walt Whitman heard many of the different voices that make America sing. On the next page you will read about one person who felt his voice had not been heard.*

Source: Walt Whitman, *Leaves of Grass*. Brooklyn, NY: Fowler and Wells, 1856.

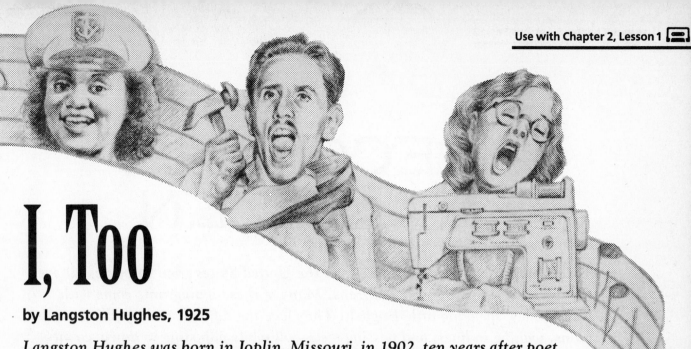

# I, Too

**by Langston Hughes, 1925**

*Langston Hughes was born in Joplin, Missouri, in 1902, ten years after poet Walt Whitman's death. Hughes grew up admiring Whitman's poetry about ordinary people. However, Hughes felt that one group's "songs" were not being heard: African Americans. So in 1925 Hughes sat down and wrote his own poem, "I, Too." How would you compare Walt Whitman's and Langston Hughes's views of America?*

I, too, sing America.
I am the darker brother.
They send me to eat in the kitchen
When company comes,
But I laugh,
And eat well,
And grow strong.
Tomorrow,
I'll be at the table
When company comes.
Nobody'll dare
Say to me,
"Eat in the kitchen,"
Then.
Besides,
They'll see how beautiful I am
And be ashamed—
I, too, am America.

*Langston Hughes's poem became as famous as Walt Whitman's. But many people had to work for civil rights to make Hughes's hope for "tomorrow" come true.*

Source: Langston Hughes, *Collected Poems* by Langston Hughes. New York: Alfred A. Knopf, 1994.

# BECOMING A CITIZEN

*Today immigrants continue to come to the United States from countries all over the world, seeking to become citizens. Many of these immigrants come with little money, speaking little English. They face the difficult task of filling out forms, waiting in lines, and passing tests—all while adjusting to a new country. To most, it seems like a small price to pay to live in the country of their choice.*

*To make the process of becoming a citizen easier, the United States government has printed a book that explains the forms the immigrants must fill out and has samples of the test they must take. Look at the samples on the next page. What do you think it feels like to be an immigrant hoping to become a citizen?*

*Elio Reyes is a fourth-grade student in Houston. He came to Houston with his parents and his sister Teresa from Monterrey, Mexico, in 1993. Elio says, "I miss my grandparents, cousins, and uncles back in Mexico and I miss all the festivals with parades."*

*But Elio is very happy to be in the United States. "I like my school, especially the computers, and I found a new food I never tasted before I came here—hamburgers. I really like them." Elio looks forward to becoming a citizen of the United States. He hopes to be a police officer so he can protect people from crime.*

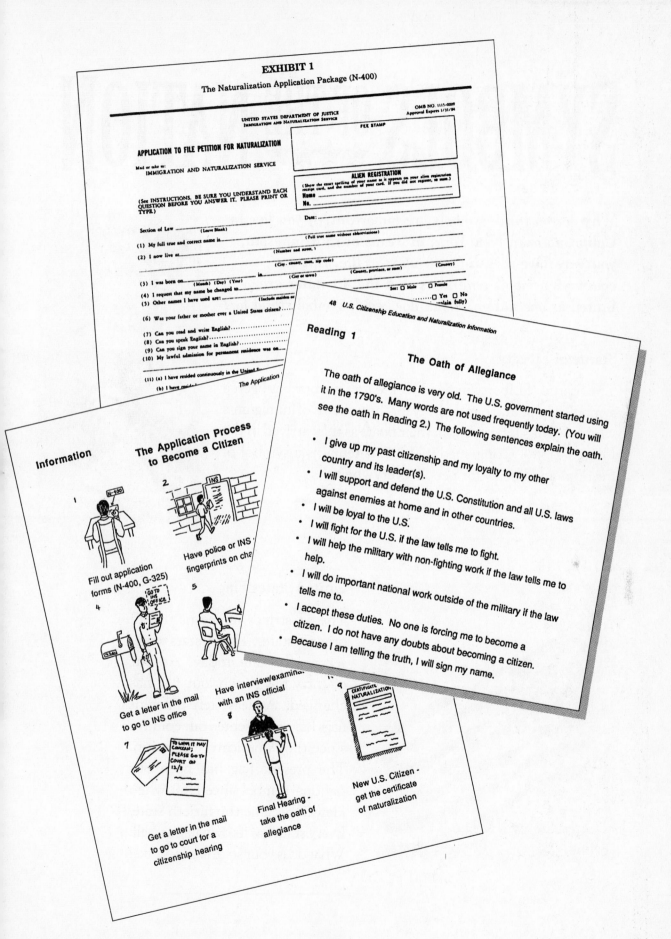

# EXHIBIT 1

## The Naturalization Application Package (N-400)

UNITED STATES DEPARTMENT OF JUSTICE
IMMIGRATION AND NATURALIZATION SERVICE

OMB NO. 1115-0009
Approval Expires 1/31/94

FEE STAMP

### APPLICATION TO FILE PETITION FOR NATURALIZATION

Mail or take to:
IMMIGRATION AND NATURALIZATION SERVICE

(See INSTRUCTIONS. BE SURE YOU UNDERSTAND EACH
QUESTION BEFORE YOU ANSWER IT. PLEASE PRINT OR
TYPE.)

**ALIEN REGISTRATION**
(Show the exact spelling of your name as it appears on your alien registration
receipt card, and the number of your card. If you did not register, so state.)
Name ......................
No. ......................
Date: ......................

Section of Law .............. (Leave Blank)

(1) My full true and correct name is............... (Full true name without abbreviations)

(2) I now live at............... (Number and street, )
............... (City, county, state, zip code)

(3) I was born on............... (Month) (Day) (Year) in............... (City or town) ............... (County, province, or state) ............... (Country)

(4) I request that my name be changed to...............  Sex: ☐ Male  ☐ Female

(5) Other names I have used are: ............... (Include maiden n...

(6) Was your father or mother ever a United States citizen?............... ☐ Yes ☐ No ...plain fully)

(7) Can you read and write English?...............

(8) Can you speak English?...............

(9) Can you sign your name in English?...............

(10) My lawful admission for permanent residence was on...............

(11) (a) I have resided continuously in the United S...

(b) I have resid...

The Application...

---

## Information — The Application Process to Become a Citizen

1. Fill out application forms (N-400, G-325)

2. Have police or INS take fingerprints on cha...

4. Get a letter in the mail to go to INS office

5. Have interview/examina... with an INS official

7. Get a letter in the mail to go to court for a citizenship hearing

8. Final Hearing - take the oath of allegiance

9. New U.S. Citizen - get the certificate of naturalization

---

## Reading 1

### The Oath of Allegiance

The oath of allegiance is very old. The U.S. government started using it in the 1790's. Many words are not used frequently today. (You will see the oath in Reading 2.) The following sentences explain the oath.

- I give up my past citizenship and my loyalty to my other country and its leader(s).
- I will support and defend the U.S. Constitution and all U.S. laws against enemies at home and in other countries.
- I will be loyal to the U.S.
- I will fight for the U.S. if the law tells me to fight.
- I will help the military with non-fighting work if the law tells me to help.
- I will do important national work outside of the military if the law tells me to.
- I accept these duties. No one is forcing me to become a citizen. I do not have any doubts about becoming a citizen.
- Because I am telling the truth, I will sign my name.

# SYMBOLS OF THE NATION

*Why do you think symbols are important? If you live in California or in New York, in Texas or in Minnesota, you may have very different ways of life. But our country's symbols remind us that the 50 states are united as one nation. What does each symbol stand for?*

**Statue of Liberty**

The Statue of Liberty in New York City's harbor has been a symbol of hope and opportunity for the millions of immigrants who saw "Miss Liberty" from their boats as they arrived in the United States. Completed in 1886, it remains a symbol of freedom and liberty for people everywhere.

**United States Flag**

The 13 stripes represent the 13 original states. The 50 stars represent each state today. As our country has grown, our flag has changed. At least ten different flags have represented our country since the American Revolution. The present flag has been our national symbol since 1960, when Hawaii became the fiftieth state. Every state has its own flag as well. What does your state flag look like?

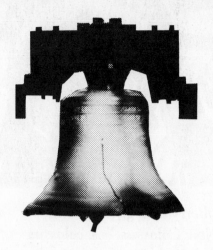

### Liberty Bell

Like the Statue of Liberty, the Liberty Bell is a symbol of freedom. It hung in Independence Hall in Philadelphia where the Declaration of Independence and the United States Constitution were written. It rang on July 4, 1776, to celebrate our first Independence Day.

### Great Seal of the United States

Does this seal look familiar? You see it every time you look at a $1 bill. Designed over 200 years ago, the Great Seal of the United States is also found on many documents signed by the President. The American bald eagle is in the center. In one claw is an olive branch, symbolizing peace. In the other are 13 arrows, representing the strength of the 13 original states. The words *E Pluribus Unum* are Latin for "out of many, one." Out of many people, and many states, one united country is formed.

*These are just some of the symbols that represent our country and our government. Can you think of any others? Suppose you had to design a symbol for your state. What ideas would you consider?*

# THE NEW COLOSSUS

**by Emma Lazarus, 1883**

*When France gave the United States the Statue of Liberty as a gift in 1880, Emma Lazarus was moved to write the poem "The New Colossus." A colossus is something gigantic. Emma Lazarus was born in New York City in 1849. As a young woman she saw both her city and the United States change with the constant flow of immigrants from other countries. Many arrived penniless, carrying just a bundle of clothing. But they also came with great dreams of starting a new life in a new land. Whom is the Statue of Liberty welcoming?*

Not like the **brazen** giant of Greek fame,
With **conquering** limbs **astride** from land to land;
Here at our sea-washed, sunset gates shall stand
A mighty woman with a torch, whose flame
Is the **imprisoned** lightning, and her name
Mother of **Exiles**. From her **beacon-hand**
Glows world-wide welcome; her mild eyes command
The air-bridged harbor that twin cities frame.

"Keep, ancient lands, your **storied pomp**!" cries she
With silent lips. "Give me your tired, your poor,
Your **huddled masses** yearning to breathe free,
The **wretched refuse** of your **teeming** shore.
Send these, the homeless, **tempest-tost** to me,
I lift my lamp beside the golden door!"

**brazen:** bold

**conquering:** mighty

**astride:** with one leg on each side

**imprisoned:** captured

**exiles:** people forced out of their countries

**beacon-hand:** hand that holds a guiding light

**storied pomp:** old habits and fancy ways

**huddled masses:** crowds of poor people

**wretched refuse:** unwanted people

**teeming:** crowded

**tempest-tost:** battered by storms

*"The New Colossus" was carved into a bronze plaque and mounted at the base of the Statue of Liberty when the statue was completed in 1886. Today the statue still welcomes people coming to the United States through New York Harbor. The statue symbolizes hope and freedom to millions of people throughout the world.*

Source: Emma Lazarus, *Poems of Emma Lazarus*. Boston: Houghton-Mifflin Company, 1889.

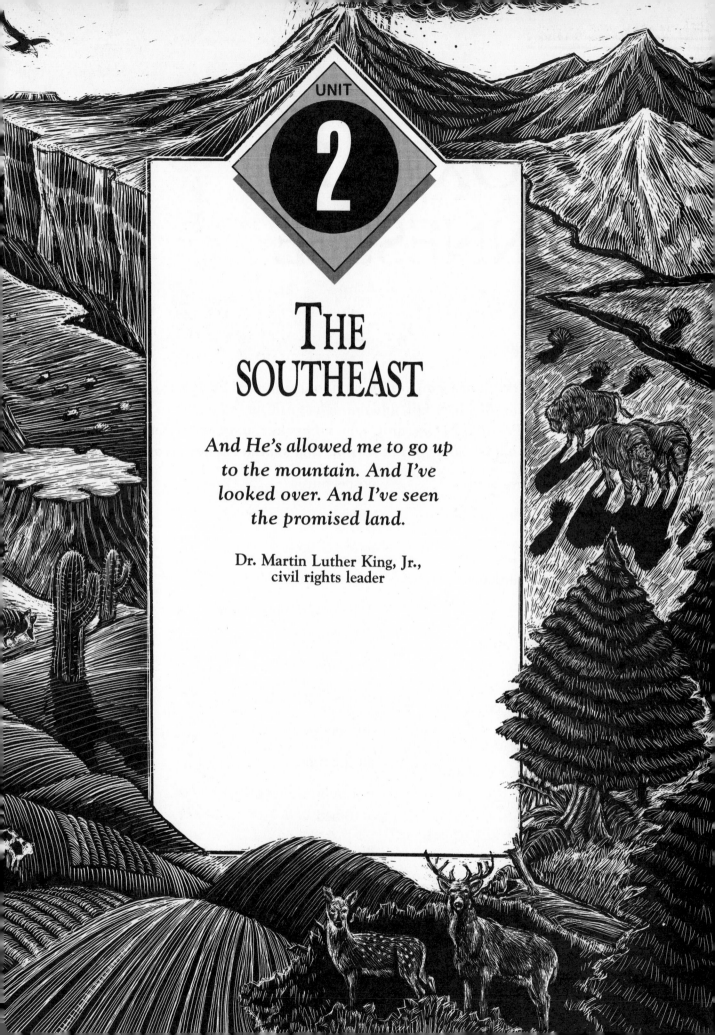

# 2

# THE SOUTHEAST

*And He's allowed me to go up to the mountain. And I've looked over. And I've seen the promised land.*

**Dr. Martin Luther King, Jr.,**
civil rights leader

# KNOXVILLE, TENNESSEE

## by Nikki Giovanni

*What do you think of when you think about summer? Perhaps you think of vacation, swimming, baseball, and enough sunshine to be able to play outdoors after dinner. Poet Nikki Giovanni remembers her summers in Knoxville, Tennessee. What are some of the reasons that summer is her favorite season?*

I always like summer

best

you can eat fresh corn

from daddy's garden

and okra

and greens

and cabbage

and lots of barbecue

and buttermilk

and homemade ice cream

at the church picnic

and listen to

gospel music

outside

at the church

homecoming

and go to the mountains
   with

your grandmother

and go barefooted

and be warm

all the time

not only when you go
   to bed

and sleep

*Which season do you like best? If you wrote a poem about that season, what things would you include?*

Source: Nikki Giovanni, *Black Feeling Black Talk Black Judgement*. New York: William Morrow & Company, Inc., 1968.

# When I Was Young in the Mountains

## by Cynthia Rylant

*Cynthia Rylant grew up in the Appalachian Mountains, in Cool Ridge, West Virginia. Her grandfather was a coal miner, and they lived in a small house with no running water. Times may have been tough, but her memories are of a simple, happy life. Rylant remembers little things with great joy, like swimming in a swimming hole and pumping water from a well. Her memories are from a different time, the 1950s. Many things have changed since the time that Rylant remembers. But life in the Appalachian Mountains is still different from life in a city. How do you think that living in the mountains affects a person's way of life?*

When I was young in the mountains, Grandfather came home in the evening covered with the black dust of a coal mine. Only his lips were clean, and he used them to kiss the top of my head.

When I was young in the mountains, Grandmother spread the table with hot corn bread, pinto beans and fried okra. Later, in the middle of the night, she walked through the grass with me to the **johnny-house** and held my hand in the dark. I promised never to eat more than one serving of okra again.

**johnny-house:** an outdoor bathroom

When I was young in the mountains, we walked across the cow pasture and through the woods, carrying our towels. The swimming hole was dark and muddy, and we sometimes saw snakes, but we jumped in anyway. On our way home, we stopped at Mr. Crawford's for a mound of white butter. Mr. Crawford and Mrs. Crawford looked alike and always smelled of sweet milk.

When I was young in the mountains, we pumped pails of water from the well at the bottom of the hill, and heated the water to fill round tin tubs for our baths. Afterwards we stood in front of the old black stove, shivering and giggling, while Grandmother heated cocoa on top.

When I was young in the mountains, we went to church in the schoolhouse on Sundays, and sometimes walked with the **congregation** through the cow pasture to the dark swimming hole, for **baptism**. My cousin Peter was laid back into the water, and his white shirt stuck to him, and my Grandmother cried.

**congregation:** church group

**baptism:** a religious ceremony in which a person is dipped into water

When I was young in the mountains,
we listened to frogs sing at dusk and
awoke to cowbells outside our windows.
Sometimes a black snake came in the yard,
and my Grandmother would threaten it with
a hoe. If it did not leave, she used the hoe to kill
it. Four of us once **draped** a very long snake, dead
of course, across our necks for a photograph.

**hoe:** long tool used
for loosening soil
**draped:** hung

When I was young in the mountains, we sat on the porch
swing in the evenings, and Grandfather sharpened my pencils
with his pocket knife. Grandmother sometimes shelled beans
and sometimes braided my hair. The dogs lay around us, and
the stars sparkled in the sky. A bob white whistled in the forest.
Bob-bob-bob white!

When I was young in the mountains, I never wanted to go
to the ocean, and I never wanted to go the desert. I never
wanted to go anywhere else in the world, for I was in the
mountains. And that was always enough.

*Today you may swim in a pool and get your water from a faucet. But you may
also find pleasure in simple things. What are some of the things you enjoy about
your everyday life? How do you think you'll describe them to younger people
when you grow up?*

Source: Cynthia Rylant, *When I Was Young in the Mountains.* New York: E. P. Dutton, 1982.

# John Henry

**Traditional Ballad**

*In addition to coal, steel has played an important role in the economy of the Southeast. In 1869 the eastern and western parts of the United States were connected by railroad. Thousands of miles of railroad tracks were laid down by strong workers like the legendary John Henry, a steel driller in the early 1870s. During this period, railroad companies began using machines to do some of the work. The story has it that John Henry died trying to beat a steam drill in a race to dig the Big Bend Tunnel in West Virginia. Songs and stories describing John Henry's strength and courage spread across the country. Why do you think it was so important to John Henry to beat the machine?*

1. When John Hen - ry was ____ a lit - tle
2. Now the cap - tain said ____ to John ____
3. John ____ Hen - ry told ____ his ____
4. John ____ Hen - ry ham - mered on the
5. They ____ took John Hen - ry to the

ba - by   Sit - ting on ____ his ____ pap - py's ____
Hen - ry,   "I'm ____ gon - na bring that steam ____ drill a -
cap - tain,   "A ____ man ____ ain't ____ noth - ing but a
moun - tain,   Till his ham - mer ____ was ____ strik - ing
grave - yard,   And they bur - ied ____ him ____ in the

Source: Edith Fowke and Joe Glazer, *Songs of Work and Protest*. New York: Dover Publications, 1973.

# In Coal Country

## by Judith Hendershot

*Coal is an important natural resource. It can be used to make electricity, to manufacture steel, and to provide heat. For many people who lived in Coal Country—Ohio, Pennsylvania, and West Virginia—in the 1930s and 1940s, coal mining was a way of life. Families lived close together in communities called coal camps. Judith Hendershot, whose father and grandfathers were miners, drew from her parents' memories of a coal camp called Willow Grove to write this book. What was it like to grow up in a coal-mining community?*

Papa dug coal from deep in the earth to earn a living. He dressed for work when everyone else went to bed. He wore faded **denims** and steel-toed shoes and he walked a mile to his job at the mine every night. He carried a silver lunch bucket and had a light on his miner's hat. It was important work. He was proud to do it.

**denims:** jeans

In the morning I listened for the whistle that signaled the end of the **hoot-owl shift**. Sometimes I walked up the run to meet Papa. He was always covered with **grime** and dirt, but I could see the whites of his eyes smiling at me. He let me carry his silver lunch bucket.

**hoot-owl shift:** night working time

**grime:** greasy dirt

When we got home, Mama took the number three tub from where it hung on the back porch and filled it with water heated on the huge iron stove. She **draped** a blanket across one corner of the kitchen and Papa washed off the coal dust. We got a bath only on Saturdays, but Papa had one every day. Then Papa went to bed and we went to school.

We lived in a place called the Company Row. The ten white houses sat in a straight line. They were built by the people who owned the Black Diamond Mine. Two miners' families lived side by side in each two-story house. Seventy-five children lived and played there in the Row. We had many friends.

Outside, our houses never looked clean or painted. Coal was burned in the furnaces to heat the houses and in the stoves to cook the food. The stove fires sent smoke and soot up the chimneys. The smoke had a **disagreeable** smell, and something in it made the paint peel off the houses. Tiny specks of soot floated out and covered everything.

Our coal camp was called Willow Grove. The houses were **huddled** in a **hollow** between two softly rising hills. In the spring the hills were covered with **lady's-slippers** and yellow and white violets. Mama always had a jar of spring flowers on the kitchen table. Weeping willow trees lined the banks of the creek that flowed behind the Company Row.

The water in the creek was often black. The coal was dragged out of the mine in small cars pulled by mules. Then it was sent up into a tall building called the tipple, where it was sorted and washed. The water that washed the coal ran into the creek, and the dust from the coal turned it black as night.

Papa sometimes worked at the picking table on the tipple to sort out rocks from the good coal. After it was sorted, the good coal was dumped into railroad cars waiting under the tipple. The rest of the stone and dirt was hauled away to a gob pile. There were gob piles all over Willow Grove. The kids from the Row ran to the tops of the piles to play king of the mountain.

Sometimes a gob pile caught fire. It **smouldered** for a long time, maybe for days, and it smelled awful. When the fire went out, the stone and ash that was left was called red dog. Our roads were made of the sharp red-dog stone.

**draped:** hung

**disagreeable:** bad

**huddled:** grouped closely together
**hollow:** small valley
**lady's slippers:** flowers with a petal that looks like a shoe

**smouldered:** burned and smoked with little or no flame

Trains moved the coal in cars from the mine to the power plants and steel mills on the Ohio River. The train tracks ran alongside the Company Row. We watched from the porch swing as the **engineer** worked his **levers** to guide the train, blowing clouds of hot white steam on the tracks. One engine pushed and another pulled as many as one hundred cars at a time. The houses shook as the trains rumbled by.

**engineer:** train driver
**levers:** handles

The coal cars moved all through the day and into the night. Sometimes in the middle of the night we heard the clang of steel as the cars were **hitched** to the engine. Often the load was too much for the engine. It groaned. The tracks creaked. The wheels screeched as the brakeman spread sand on the rails to get the cars moving. Then the train began to move very slowly, and we could hear the wheels straining a slow "Chug-a-chug, chug-a-chug." Later in the distance, the engine's whistle moaned a familiar cry. "Whoo-whoo."

**hitched:** attached

In the morning we took buckets and gathered the lumps of coal that had rolled off the cars in the struggle of the night before.

The **vibration** of the trains often made the rails on the tracks come apart. When that happened, the paddy man came to repair the tracks. He rode a **flatcar**, which he pedaled by himself. While he worked to replace the **spikes** in the rails, the paddy man sang:

**vibration:** shaking

**flatcar:** railroad car with a flat platform and no sides
**spikes:** large, heavy nails

*"Paddy on the railroad,*
*Paddy on the sea.*
*Paddy ripped his pants,*
*And he blamed it on me."*

Mama worked hard like Papa. She planted our garden and she canned vegetables for the winter. She stored her quart jars of beans and tomatoes and peas in the **earthen** room in the cellar. Every other day Mama baked her special rye bread in the oven of the iron stove. We often ate the bread right out of the oven with fried potatoes and sliced tomatoes.

> **earthen:** made of baked clay

Washing the clothes was a long, hard job. We carried the wash water from the pump down by the creek. Mama heated the water in a copper boiler on her huge stove. She scrubbed the clothes on a washboard with a stiff brush. Her hands were red and wrinkled when she was finished.

In the summer, when it was hot, the Company Row kids often climbed the hills above the grove. We cooled ourselves by standing under Bernice Falls. The water flowed from a natural spring on the **ridge** above. It was cool and clean and it tasted so sweet.

> **ridge:** a long, narrow, raised strip of land

We walked the red-dog road to the Company Store. Anything the miners' families needed, from matches to **pongee** dresses, could be found there. Every payday Papa treated us to an **Eskimo Pie**.

The Company Row kids played hopscotch in the dirt. Our favorite game was **mumbletypeg**. In the evenings we built bonfires along the creek and roasted potatoes on willow sticks.

> **pongee:** a soft, thin cloth made of silk
> **Eskimo Pie:** vanilla ice-cream bar covered with chocolate
> **mumbletypeg:** an old game in which players try to throw a knife so the blade sticks in the ground

In the autumn the hills were ablaze with color. We gathered hickory nuts and butternuts and dragged them home in burlap sacks. Papa shelled them and spread them on the porch roof to dry. Mama used the nutmeats in cookies at holiday time.

In the winter we climbed from the hollow to Baker's Ridge. Our sleds were made from leftover tin used for roofs, and we rode them down through the woods by moonlight. When the black creek was frozen, we shared a few skates and everyone took a turn. When we got home, we hung our wet clothes over the stove to dry and warmed ourselves in Mama's kitchen.

Christmas in the row was the best time of the year. Papa cut a fresh tree up on the ridge, and we pulled it home on a tin sled. Mama placed a candle on the end of each branch. The tree was lighted once, on Christmas Eve. Papa spent the whole day **basting** the roast goose for Mama. Our stockings bulged with tangerines and nuts and hard cinnamon candies. The house smelled of Christmas tree and roast goose and all the good things that Mama had made. No whistle called Papa to the mine. Everything felt so special. And it was.

**basting:** adding a sauce to food while roasting

*Coal is still an important resource. But the burning of coal can cause air pollution. Today people are looking for better ways to burn coal more cleanly and cheaply. As natural resources such as petroleum and natural gas get used up, we may need to depend on coal more and more in the future. This need will keep coal towns like Willow Grove from disappearing.*

Source: Judith Hendershot, *In Coal Country.* New York: Knopf, 1987.

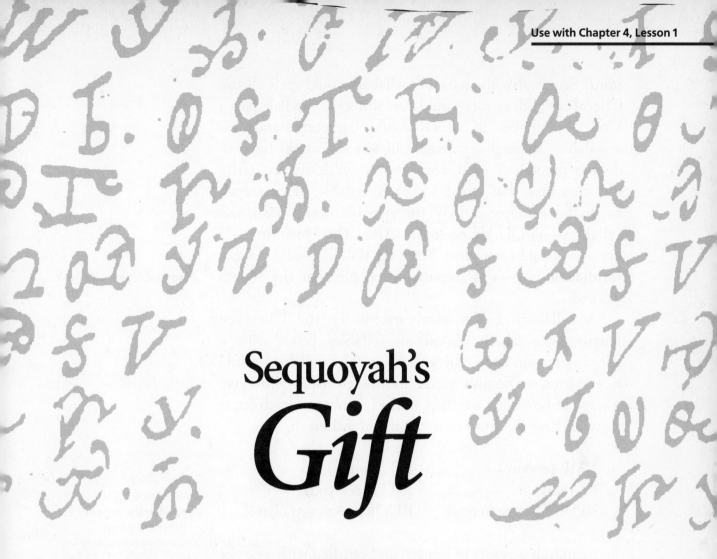

# Sequoyah's
# *Gift*

## by Janet Klausner

*Sequoyah lived at a time when his people, the Cherokee, were beginning to adopt many of the ways of their new neighbors in the Southeast of the young United States. Some of these changes were good, Sequoyah thought, but others were troubling. He did not want to see the Cherokee completely give up their old ways. He also did not want to see them lose their language—a language whose words had never been written down. Sequoyah began to dedicate himself to inventing a system for writing the Cherokee language. Many people thought he was crazy to spend so much time alone, scribbling symbols on paper. In this selection from a biography, we learn how Sequoyah made it possible for the Cherokee to record their history for all to read. Why do you think it took people some time to accept Sequoyah's system?*

It was 1821. Sequoyah was putting in place the last pieces of the language puzzle. He had worked on reducing two hundred different characters to a more manageable 86 (which would later be simplified to 85). Many of the characters now resembled shapes he had seen in English

37

print. Sequoyah's 86-character syllabary could spell all the Cherokee words anyone could ever think of. A syllabary is a kind of alphabet in which each character stands for a syllable. To send a message, all anyone would have to do was pronounce each word somewhat slowly and write the character that stood for each syllable. If Sequoyah wrote, for example, **DIhW** the symbols would speak the syllables—*ah-QUAH-nee-tah*. And the meaning—"I know"—would come clear. The only task left—and it was a **formidable** one—was convincing people that the system worked.

**formidable:** very difficult

A syllabary is the ideal system for the Cherokee language, in which almost all syllables begin with a consonant sound and end with a vowel. A syllabary would not do for most English words, but the few listed below give a sense of how such a system works (pronounce each letter name to hear the word or words in parentheses):

| | |
|---|---|
| NME (enemy) | MT (empty) |
| EZ (easy) | ICU (I see you) |
| XPDNC (**expediency**) | RUOK? (Are you okay?) |

**expediency:** concern for personal gain

Sequoyah was sure of himself and satisfied with what he had done. In Willstown he made a visit to the home of his cousin Ah-gee-lee, who was now the town chief. Ah-gee-lee had heard about Sequoyah's writing and asked him how he was getting on.

"I am getting on very well," Sequoyah replied. "I can write down anything I have heard. I then put it aside. I take it up again days later and there find all that I heard exactly as I heard it."

"It may be that you are not forgetful," his cousin suggested. "Your understanding of the message may come not from the marks you have invented, but from what these marks lead you to remember." Perhaps the marks merely helped Sequoyah to form **associations**, like someone trained to interpret the patterns on a **wampum belt**. Such a person could make long memorized speeches based on what those patterns suggested.

**associations:** connected thoughts

**wampum belt:** belt of small, polished beads made from shells, used by some Native American groups as money

"The same marks will make me remember very different things, according to the way in which I place them." Sequoyah said. He described how after he had written something he always put it aside and gave it no further thought. "I do not remember what I have written. But at any time afterward, I can pick up the paper and recall everything."

Ah-gee-lee remained **skeptical**. Soon afterward, when Ah-gee-lee was on a visit to Sequoyah's home, Sequoyah proudly called to his young daughter, Ah-yo-kah. She was a small child, perhaps as young as six. When she came to her father's side, he held a copy of his syllabary out to her and asked her to **recite** from it. Quickly—she had enjoyed playing this game with her father before—she pronounced the series of syllables. "Yah!" Ah-gee-lee exclaimed with astonishment. "It sounds like the Creek language."

"But the sounds, put together, make Cherokee words," Sequoyah explained. He then wrote out characters that Ah-yo-kah pronounced in sequence. She was speaking Cherokee words! Ah-gee-lee was amazed. But he was no longer doubtful. He had seen and heard for himself that Sequoyah's writing system worked.

Ah-yo-kah was one of Sequoyah's first pupils. She mastered the system easily. Sequoyah's brother-in-law was another early learner. Sequoyah's nephew learned, too. It was one thing to find relatives who would accept the syllabary, but quite another to win acceptance in the Nation.

It was when Sequoyah made a legal claim at Indian Court that others began to notice his achievement. Sequoyah came prepared with a written account of his case. When he read aloud from the page, in Cherokee, he was doing something that his listeners had never seen or heard before.

The next day a man called Big Rattling Gourd came to Sequoyah. He had witnessed Sequoyah's reading. "I could not sleep last night," Big Rattling Gourd said. "Yesterday by daylight what you did did not seem remarkable. But when night came, it was different. All night long I wondered at it and could not sleep."

**skeptical:** doubting

**recite:** read aloud

Big Rattling Gourd had been kept awake by the sudden understanding of what Sequoyah's syllabary could do. It was something to marvel at. "This **surpasses** anything I ever thought possible for a man to accomplish," Big Rattling Gourd said.

**surpasses:** is greater than

Sequoyah explained that he had done it for a good purpose, even though everyone thought he was injuring himself and his family.

Big Rattling Gourd asked Sequoyah one question after another. "Can you write anything you choose? Or must it be only particular things?"

Sequoyah replied that he could write anything at all, provided it was spoken in Cherokee. "If it is in any other language, I cannot write it."

"I remember the chiefs of the past and the speeches they made. If I repeat those speeches to you, will you be able to write them down?" Big Rattling Gourd felt it was important that these speeches be recorded faithfully. At councils, speakers quoted from these speeches, but he knew that their quotations were not always accurate.

Sequoyah explained that this was one of the uses of the syllabary. Anyone who had memory of an important speech or event could now find a way to **preserve** it for all time.

**preserve:** save

When Big Rattling Gourd left, his mind was filled with possibilities for this **wondrous** invention.

**wondrous:** wonderful

*Sequoyah's gift was indeed a huge accomplishment for one person. What is a syllabary? How is it different from the English alphabet?*

Source: Janet Klausner, *Sequoyah's Gift: A Portrait of the Cherokee Leader.* New York: HarperCollins, 1993.

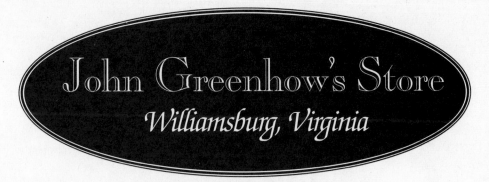

## by Ron and Nancy Goor

*General stores were an important part of colonial life. In these shops people could buy whatever they could not make themselves. Most of these items were imported from Europe. In Williamsburg, the capital of the Virginia Colony, many items came from England. Although the colonists wanted America to be imdependent, Americans could not yet manufacture all the things they needed and wanted. On the next page you can see a photograph of John Greenhow's store from present-day "Colonial Williamsburg." The people in the photograph are actors helping visitors to understand what life was like in colonial times. What items are for sale in the store?*

Stores such as John Greenhow's were stocked with **a multitude of** imported goods. You could buy your quills, ink powder and note books, Irish **linens**, fashionable buttons, smoothing irons, ready-made shirts . . . iron kettles, sponges, brooms, and tools for almost every occasion.

**a multitude of:** many

**linens:** household items made of cloth, such as sheets and towels

At Greenhow's you could purchase anything you might need or just enjoyed having. However you had to use ready money (Spanish or Dutch coins). Mr. Greenhow accepted no credit. A popular form of money in the Virginia colony was notes of credit made with London tobacco merchants and other kinds of promises to pay. Virginia colonists were forced to use these types of currency because England would not allow them to mint their own coins or to use English ones. Often they resorted to **barter**. A housewife might pay for a bag of sugar with a dozen eggs. When they could, townspeople bought on credit and took years to pay.

**barter:** trade

Joseph West
BOOT & SHOEMAKER,
WILLIAMSBURG, VIRGINIA,
hereby acquaints the Publick that
he has opened Shop on the main
Street near the Travis House,
where he carries on the SHOE-
MAKING Business in all its
Branches.

...feph Kobelbauer,
...Cabinet-Maker.
...yscough's Old Shop in the
...pitol Square, Williams-
...g, Virginia
...KES and repairs FUR-
...TURE of every De-
...n the finest Manner, &
...me Any that care to
...Work in the Under-
...Goods will be sold
...P, but may be had
...m his Agents elsewhere.

Other kinds of stores were also important in colonial Williamsburg. The milliner's shop offered locally-made hats and imported clothes. At the silversmith's, colonists could buy small objects like spoons or have their silver coins made into serving pieces for safer keeping. And men could always visit the wig maker's to find wigs in the latest fashion. (Women wore their hair curled.) Above you can see posters advertising shops run by two other Williamsburg craftsmen. What services do they offer?

Source: Ron and Nancy Goor, *Williamsburg: Cradle of the Revolution*. New York: Atheneum, 1994.

# THE BRAVE CONDUCTOR

## by Virginia Hamilton

*Harriet Tubman was born into slavery on a plantation in Maryland in 1820. From the age of six, she chopped wood and hoed fields with the other enslaved people. When Harriet was around 11 years old she began to hear other slaves whispering about an "Underground Railroad," an escape road to the North. In 1848 Harriet Tubman escaped to freedom on the Underground Railroad, but she returned south again and again to guide others to liberty. Virginia Hamilton writes books for children about the history and experiences of African Americans. In this selection from* Many Thousand Gone, *Hamilton retells the biography of Harriet Tubman, including some details you may not have heard before. Why do you think Tubman was willing to risk her life to bring freedom to others?*

**S**he was called the greatest conductor on the Underground Railroad. Slaves named her Moses because, like the biblical Moses, she led her "travelers" from **bondage** to freedom. Araminta was the name given her, which she changed to Harriet after her mother. She was born into slavery in about 1820 in Dorchester County, Maryland, one of Harriet and Benjamin Ross's eleven children. As a

**bondage:** slavery

43

slave child Harriet grew up with little time for play and no schooling. Instead, she had plenty of work and many beatings by her owner.

Sometime during her youth, Harriet Ross was hit on the head by a heavy weight thrown by her owner. The severe blow caused her to fall asleep whenever she was quiet for longer than fifteen minutes. She thus became physically active to keep herself awake.

As she grew older, Harriet did not often live with her owner; he hired her out to work for various people. This was a common practice in those times; when an owner no longer needed the services of one of his slaves, he rented the slave out to someone who did.

When she was in her twenties, word reached Harriet that she and two of her brothers were to be sold. She ran away, believing she had a right to liberty or death. "One or the other I mean to have," she said. She made a successful escape and found her way into free Pennsylvania.

Once free, Harriet stared at her hands to see if she was the same person out of slavery as she had been in it. She surely felt different. "There was such a glory over everything," she said. "The sun come like gold through the trees."

Unfortunately, Harriet had to leave behind her brothers and her husband, John Tubman, who had said he would report her if she ran.

Later she did go back for him, but he had already remarried. As John Tubman **seeped** out of her wounded heart, the woman known to history as Harriet Tubman devoted herself to the freeing of others.

**seeped:** flowed slowly

She went about establishing a **network** of Underground stations from the South all the way into Canada, making more than twenty dangerous journeys into the South to do so. She returned for her brothers and brought them out. She took her elderly mother and father north. Over her lifetime, Harriet Tubman brought out more than three hundred slaves along the Underground Railroad. Rewards for her capture, posted by the slave owners from whom she liberated slaves, finally reached the sum of

**network:** connected system

$40,000. But Harriet thought of everything. She hired someone to follow the man who posted descriptions of runaways. Once the man left the area, Harriet's assistant tore the posters down....

Harriet Tubman became a heroine to the **abolitionists**. Northern antislavery leaders such as Thomas Garrett were always eager to help her with food, money, or **lodging**. She herself helped abolitionist John Brown (who called her General Tubman) in **recruiting** men for the **uprising** he led at Harpers Ferry.

In the 1850s, Harriet appeared at many antislavery meetings and also began speaking out on women's rights. Because of the huge price on her head, she was forced to flee to Canada just before the start of the Civil War. But she did return to America in 1862, and served as a spy, **scout**, and nurse for the Union Army in North Carolina.

After the war, she turned her home into the Home for **Indigent** and Aged Negroes, which supported freedpeople. She married Nelson Davis, a war veteran, in 1869.

Harriet Tubman lived out much of her old age in poverty. Then, thirty years after the Civil War's end, she received a war-widow's pension of $20 a month for the rest of her life. So **humane** was she that she used nearly all of the money to maintain her home, later known as the Harriet Tubman Home, as a **refuge** for the needy. She died in 1913, at the age of ninety-three.

**abolitionists:** people who wanted to end slavery

**lodging:** a place to stay

**recruiting:** getting the services of

**uprising:** revolt

**scout:** someone sent out to gather information

**indigent:** poor

**humane:** kind

**refuge:** shelter, place of protection

*Even as an elderly woman, Tubman continued to help others. What impresses you most about her story?*

Source: Virginia Hamilton, *Many Thousand Gone: African Americans from Slavery to Freedom.* New York: Alfred A. Knopf, Inc., 1993.

# BATTLE CRY OF FREEDOM

### Civil War Battle Song

**Northern Version by George F. Root, 1861**     **Southern Version by W. H. Barnes, 1861**

*When the Civil War began in 1861, songwriters rushed to write songs for soldiers to sing. One of the most popular songs to sweep the North was George F. Root's "Battle Cry of Freedom." Union troops sang it in camp, in battle, and when marching. The tune was so catchy that Confederate troops also began singing it—but they, of course, wanted different words. So a Southerner named W. H. Barnes wrote a new version for the South. How do the two versions reveal two different perspectives?*

Spirited

*North:*  1. Yes we'll ral - ly 'round the flag, boys, we'll
*South:*  1. Our _____ flag is proud - ly float-ing, On the

ral - ly once a - gain, Shout - ing the bat - tle cry of
land and on the main, Shout, shout the bat - tle cry of

Free - dom, We will ral - ly from the hill - side, we'll
Free - dom; Be - neath it oft we've con-quered, And will

gath - er from the plain, Shout - ing the bat - tle cry of Free - dom.
con - quer oft a - gain, Shout, shout the bat - tle cry of Free - dom.

*Chorus*

*North:*  The Un - ion for - ev - er, Hur - rah, boys, Hur - rah!
*South:*  Our Dix - ie for - ev - er, she's nev - er at a loss;

46

Down with the trai - tor, Up with the star; While we
Down with the ea - gle, Up with the cross. We'll ___

ral - ly 'round the flag, boys, Ral - ly once a - gain.
ral - ly 'round the bon-ny flag, we'll ral - ly once a - gain.

Shout - ing the bat - tle cry of Free - dom. Free - dom.
Shout, shout the bat - tle cry of Free - dom. Free - dom.

### North:

2. We are springing to the call
   Of our brothers gone before,
     Shouting the battle cry of Freedom,
   And we'll fill the vacant ranks
   With a million Free men more,
     Shouting the battle cry of Freedom.

*Chorus*

3. We will welcome to our numbers
   The loyal, true and brave,
     Shouting the battle cry of Freedom,
   And although he may be poor
   He shall never be a slave,
     Shouting the battle cry of Freedom.

*Chorus*

4. So we're springing to the call
   From the East and from the West,
     Shouting the battle cry of Freedom,
   And we'll hurl the rebel crew
   From the land we love the best,
     Shouting the battle cry of Freedom.

*Chorus*

### South:

2. Our gallant boys have marched
   To the rolling of the drums,
     Shout, shout the battle cry of Freedom;
   And the leaders in charge
   Cry, "Come boys, come!"
     Shout, shout the battle cry of Freedom.

*Chorus*

3. They have laid down their lives
   On the bloody battle field,
     Shout, shout the battle cry of Freedom;
   Their motto is resistance—
   "To tyrants we'll not yield!"
     Shout, shout the battle cry of Freedom.

*Chorus*

4. While our boys have responded
   And to the field have gone,
     Shout, shout the battle cry of Freedom;
   Our noble women also
   Have aided them at home.
     Shout, shout the battle cry of Freedom.

*Chorus*

Source: Paul Glass and Louis Singer, *Singing Soldiers: A History of the Civil War in Song.*
New York: Da Capo Press, 1975.

# Rosa Parks: My Story

**by Rosa Parks**

*For many years African Americans in the South had been forced by law to sit in separate sections of trains and buses. Most blacks opposed these unfair laws, and on December 1, 1955, a woman in Montgomery, Alabama, decided to do something about them. What did Rosa Parks do? Parks tells you herself in the following selection from her autobiography. In what ways does she show courage?*

When I got off from work that evening of December 1, I went to Court Square as usual to catch the Cleveland Avenue bus home. I didn't look to see who was driving when I got on, and by the time I recognized him, I had already paid my fare. It was the same driver who had put me off the bus back in 1943, twelve years earlier. He was still tall and heavy, with red, rough-looking skin. And he was still mean-looking. I didn't know if he had been on that route before—they switched the drivers around sometimes. I do know that most of the time if I saw him on a bus, I wouldn't get on it.

I saw a **vacant** seat in the middle section of the bus and took it. I didn't even question why there was a vacant seat even though there were quite a few people standing in the back. If I had thought about it at all, I would probably have figured maybe someone saw me get on and did not take the seat but left it vacant for me. There was a man sitting next to the window and two women across the aisle.

**vacant:** empty

The next stop was the Empire Theater, and some whites got on. They filled up the white seats, and one man was left standing. The driver looked back at us. He said, "Let me have

48

those front seats," because they were the front seats of the black section. Didn't anybody move. We just sat where we were, the four of us. Then he spoke a second time: "Y'all better **make it light** on yourselves and let me have those seats."

The man in the window seat next to me stood up, and I moved to let him pass by me, and then I looked across the aisle and saw that the two women were also standing. I moved over to the window seat. I could not see how standing up was going to "make it light" for me. The more we gave in and complied, the worse they treated us. . . .

People always say that I didn't give up my seat because I was tired, but that isn't true. I was not tired physically, or no more tired than I usually was at the end of a working day. I was not old, although some people have an image of me as being old then. I was forty-two. No, the only tired I was, was tired of giving in.

The driver of the bus saw me still sitting there, and he asked was I going to stand up. I said, "No." He said, "Well, I'm going to have you arrested." Then I said, "You may do that." These were the only words we said to each other. I didn't even know his name, which was James Blake, until we were in court together. He got out of the bus and stayed outside for a few minutes, waiting for the police.

THIS PART OF THE BUS FOR THE COLORED RACE

*In the 1950s African Americans were forced by law to sit separately, in the back of the bus.*

*Rosa Parks takes a seat where she chooses, one year after her historic protest which led to the end of segregation on public transportation.*

As I sat there, I tried not to think about what might happen. I knew that anything was possible. I could be **manhandled** or beaten. I could be arrested. People have asked me if it occurred to me then that I could be the test case the **NAACP** had been looking for. I did not think about that at all. In fact if I had let myself think too deeply about what might happen to me, I might have gotten off the bus. But I chose to remain.

**manhandled:** treated roughly

**NAACP:** National Association for the Advancement of Colored People, an organization that works for civil rights

*Rosa Parks was arrested and put into jail. Word spread quickly throughout the African American community, and people became very angry. They, too, were tired of giving in. Led by Dr. Martin Luther King, Jr., African Americans joined together and refused to ride the city buses at all. Finally, a year later, the segregation laws were changed. Rosa Parks has spent the rest of her life working for civil rights for all people. "Everyone living together in peace and harmony and love," she writes, ". . . that's the goal that we seek."*

Source: Rosa Parks, *Rosa Parks: My Story.* New York: Dial Books, 1992.

# I See the Promised Land

**by Dr. Martin Luther King, Jr., 1968**

*Rosa Parks's decision not to give up her bus seat helped give other people the courage to fight for civil rights. One of the greatest leaders of this movement was a young minister named Dr. Martin Luther King, Jr. During the 1950s and 1960s, Dr. King led many marches and demonstrations for civil rights. Like many great leaders, King faced danger from people who weren't ready for change. In 1968, King spoke about the struggles and successes he had seen. In the final part of the speech, printed below, King explains why he is no longer afraid of being killed. What do you think he means by "the promised land"?*

Well, I don't know what will happen now. We've got some difficult days ahead. But it doesn't matter with me now. Because I've been to the mountaintop. And I don't mind. Like anybody, I would like to live a long life. **Longevity** has its place. But I'm not concerned about that now. I just want to do God's will. And He's allowed me to go up to the mountain. And I've looked over. And I've seen the promised land. I may not get there with you. But I want you to know tonight, that we, as a people, will get to the promised land. And I'm happy, tonight. I'm not worried about anything. I'm not fearing any man. Mine eyes have seen the glory of the coming of the Lord.

**longevity:** living long

*While King predicted that he might be killed before his goals were reached, he could not have known the end would come so soon. The day after this speech, April 4, 1968, King was murdered, and the civil rights movement lost its greatest leader. His words, however, have helped to keep the movement alive. Do you think that we have reached King's "promised land"?*

Source: James Melvin Washington, *A Testament of Hope: The Essential Writings of Martin Luther King, Jr.* San Francisco: Harper & Row, Publishers, 1986.

# Puerto Rico

**by Eileen Figueroa**

*One of the most beautiful places in the Southeast region is the island of Puerto Rico. When Eileen Figueroa was 15 years old, she left the small town of Camuy in Puerto Rico to move to Miami with her parents. "I like it here," she says, "but Puerto Rico is for me." Eileen's poem "Puerto Rico" was printed in her high school magazine. What are some of the things she misses the most?*

Puerto Rico, isla del Caribe
La más bella es por cierto
Con sus palmares y sus vientos,
Acaricia a todo aquel
que en esta isla se encuentra.

Puerto Rico, certainly the most beautiful
Caribbean island
With palm trees and breezes,
it caresses everyone
found on the island.

Los atardeceres en mi Borinquen
son muy tranquilos y serenos
puedes oír los coquíes
cómo cantan a lo lejos.

Dusk on my island
is so very tranquil and serene
you can hear the coquís
singing in the distance.

Querido Puerto Rico
no sabes lo mucho que lo siento
El haber tenido que dejarte
para mí es un dolor immenso.

Beloved Puerto Rico
you don't know how sorry I am
Having to leave you
is still a source of great pain.

Pero sé que algún día he de volver
a esta tierra tan querida
que llenó mis días de alegrías
y que mi corazón aún no olvida.

But I know that some day
I'll return
to this cherished land
that filled my days with joy
and that my heart cannot forget.

*After she finishes high school, Eileen plans to go to college in Puerto Rico. What things would you miss if you moved to another place?*

Source: Eileen Figueroa, "Puerto Rico." Miami, FL: *Search II Magazine*, 1991.

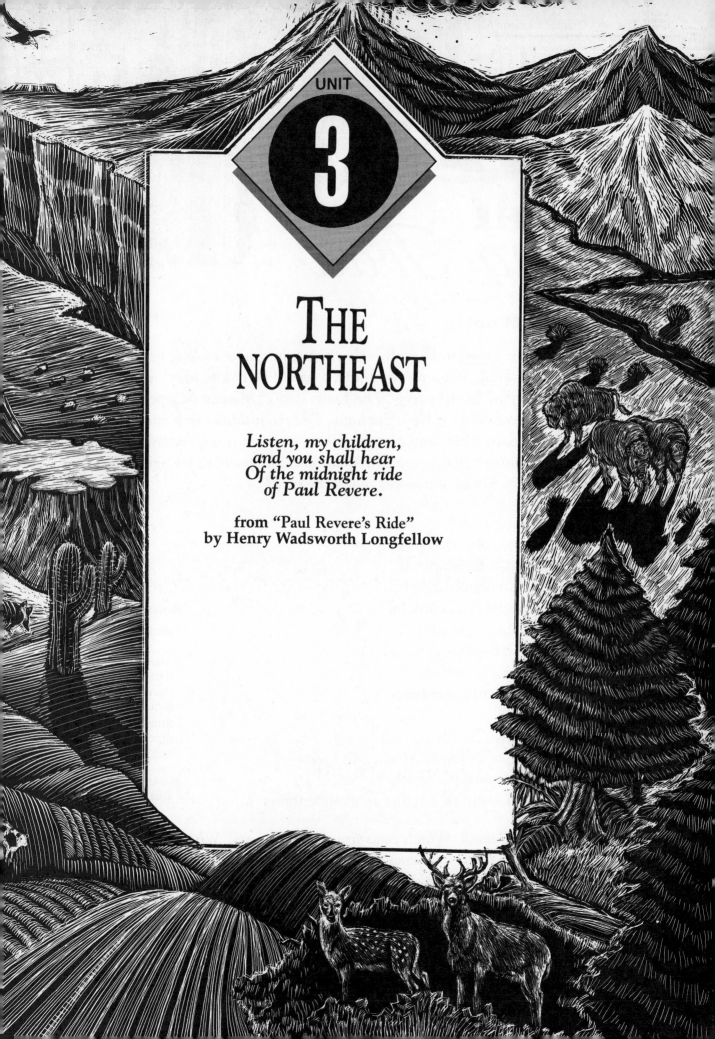

**3**

# THE NORTHEAST

*Listen, my children,
and you shall hear
Of the midnight ride
of Paul Revere.*

**from "Paul Revere's Ride"
by Henry Wadsworth Longfellow**

# THE
# *Long Trail*

## by Monica Mayper

*There are many long trails in the Northeast, but none as long as the Appalachian Trail. What do you think it would be like to hike in this wooded mountain region? In the poem "The Long Trail," Monica Mayper writes of a hike in the mountains of New England. The mountains are home to many different animals, trees, and plants. Hiking in them is a wonderful way to learn about nature and geography. What does the poet see on her climb? What surprises her as she moves along the trail?*

I climb the narrow trail
Set foot on rock, on root, on rock
Cross creekbed, follow birdcall
Through ranks of birch and pine.
My lungs take the cool, **dank** air.
A **calico** of light and shade
Plays on the fern-sprung ground.
My eyes find small surprises:
Mushrooms, **lichen, columbine**...
And then—
The sudden, unveiled sky
A green swoop of valley, all-at-once and wide—
A new **astoundment** on the other side:
More mountains, still mountains, more mountains.

**dank:** moist

**calico:** spotted pattern

**lichen:** plantlike living things growing on tree trunks, rocks, or the ground

**columbine:** showy, droopy flower with five tubelike petals

**astoundment:** amazement

*Read the poem aloud. Which lines are difficult to say? Which flow easily? In the first four lines, how does the poet make us feel the narrowness of the trail? In the last five lines, how does she help us to picture the sudden clearing? What effect does the repetition of the word mountains have at the end of the poem? Do you have a picture in your mind of the trail Mayper describes?*

Source: Loretta Krupinski, ed., *A New England Scrapbook*. New York: HarperCollins, 1994.

# FALL

### by Karla Kuskin

*Autumn in the Northeast is known for its colorful leaves and its cool, crisp weather. Some people say that this time of year "sharpens the senses." Which of the five senses does poet Karla Kuskin use most on her fall walk in this poem? Why do you think she describes her own clothing?*

When I go walking in the fall
I stop to watch the deer.
They open up their lovely eyes
And blink
And disappear.
The rabbits hop from here
To there
And in
And out
And under
While deep within the forest heart
The black bears roar like thunder.
The chipmunks gather butternuts
And hide them in a tree
Where clever squirrels
Discover them
And laugh with squirrelish glee.
My hat is green
My jacket blue
With patches on the sleeves
And as I walk
I crunch through piles
Of red and yellow leaves.

*What is autumn like where you live? Is it much like the other seasons, or is it very different? If you were to take a walk in the fall, what would you see and hear?*

Source: Karla Kuskin, *Dogs and Dragons, Trees and Dreams.* New York: Harper & Row, 1980.

# Blow, Ye Winds, in the Morning

*The harbors and bays of New England make the Northeast a rich fishing area. At one time whales were hunted in these waters. Whale fat, or blubber, was used to make oil. Later, kerosene replaced whale fat as a source of fuel. Other ways of harvesting the resources of the sea are now more common, but songs such as this one recall the whalers who sailed out of ports like New Bedford. What other Northeastern towns are mentioned in the song? Why do you think the whalers needed to be "brave"?*

Traditional
Arranged by Jerome Epstein

'Tis ad-ver-tised in Bos-ton, New York, and Buf-fa-lo, Five hun-dred brave A-mer-i-cans a-whal-ing for to go ___ sing-in', "Blow, ye winds, in the

morn - ing___ Blow, ye winds, high - O!

Clear a - way the run-ning gear and blow, boys, blow!"

2. They send you to New Bedford
   that famous whaling port,
   And give you to some land sharks
   to board
   and fit you out—singin',

   *Chorus*

3. They tell you of the clipper ships
   a-going in and out,
   And say you'll take five hundred
   whales,
   before you're six months out—
   singin',

   *Chorus*

Source: Amy L. Cohn, ed., *From Sea to Shining Sea: A Treasury of American Folklore and Folk Songs.* New York: Scholastic, 1993.

# THE WALUM OLUM

**by the Lenape-Algonquian People, 1700s**

*Almost every group of people has a story about how the world began and how its people came to live in it. The Walum Olum is a story told by the Lenape Algonkian people, an Indian group that was living in what is today Pennsylvania, New Jersey, and Delaware long before Europeans arrived. They handed this story down from generation to generation for hundreds of years. Then, some time in the 1700s, they wrote the Walum Olum in pictographs— drawings made of symbols that tell a story. Look at the selection from the Walum Olum below. Which pictographs can you guess meanings for before reading the words beside them? According to the Walum Olum, what is the explanation for the beginning of the world?*

1. At first, in that place, at all times, above the earth,

2. On the earth, an extended fog, and there the **great Manito** was.

**great Manito: great Spirit**

3. At first, forever, lost in space, everywhere, the great Manito was.

4. He made the extended land and the sky.

5. He made the sun, the moon, the stars.

6. He made them all to move evenly.

7. Then the wind blew violently, and it cleared, and the water flowed off far and strong.

8. And groups of islands grew newly, and there remained.

9. **Anew** spoke the great Manito, a manito to manitos,

**anew: again**

10. To **beings, mortals**, souls and all,

**beings, mortals: people**

11. And ever after he was a manito to men, and their grandfather.

58

12. He gave the first mother, the mother of beings.

 13. He gave the fish, he gave the turtles, he gave the beasts, he gave the birds.

 14. But an evil Manito made evil beings only, monsters.

 15. He made the flies, he made the gnats.

 16. All beings were then friendly.

 17. Truly the manitos were active and kindly

 18. To those very first men, and to those first mothers; fetched them wives,

 19. And fetched them food, when first they desired it.

 20. All had cheerful knowledge, all had leisure, all thought in gladness.

 21. But very secretly an evil being, a mighty magician, came on earth,

 22. And with him brought badness, quarreling, unhappiness.

 23. Brought bad weather, brought sickness, brought death.

 24. All this took place **of old** on the earth, beyond the great tide water, at the first.

**of old:** a long time ago

*The pictograph language helped to keep the story of the Walum Olum alive. Think of a story or something you believe in. How might you use pictographs to share your ideas with someone else?*

Source: Daniel Garrison Brinton, *The Lenape and Their Legends*. Philadelphia: Library of Aboriginal American Literature, 1884.

# Turtle's Race with Bear

## an Iroquois Tale Retold by Joseph Bruchac

*In calling the five Iroquois groups together to form the Iroquois Confederacy, the Mohawk leader Hiawatha said, "We must unite ourselves into one common band." The same values and beliefs that people draw on in choosing a form of government often appear in the stories they tell. What values of the Iroquois are shown in this traditional tale?*

**I**t was an early winter, cold enough so that the ice had frozen on all the ponds and Bear, who had not yet learned in those days that it was wiser to sleep through the **White Season**, grumbled as he walked through the woods. Perhaps he was remembering a trick another animal had played on him, perhaps he was just not in a good mood. It happened that he came to the edge of a great pond and saw Turtle there with his head sticking out of the ice.

"Hah," shouted Bear, not even giving his old friend a greeting. "What are you looking at, Slow One?"

Turtle looked at Bear. "Why do you call me slow?"

**White Season:** winter

Bear snorted. "You are the slowest of the animals. If I were to race you, I would leave you far behind." Perhaps Bear had never heard of Turtle's big race with Beaver and perhaps Bear was not remembering that Turtle, like Coyote, was an animal whose greatest speed was in his Wits. But even if he had remembered, it was too late now. Turtle had been given a chance to make what had been a boring day into an interesting one.

"My friend," Turtle said, "Let us have a race to see who is the Swiftest."

"All right," said Bear. "Where will we race?"

"We will race here at this pond and the race will be tomorrow morning when the sun is the width of one hand above the horizon. You will run along the banks of the pond and I will swim in the water."

"How can that be?" Bear said. "There is ice all over the pond."

"We will do it this way," said Turtle. "I will make holes in the ice along the side of the pond and swim under the water to each hole and stick my head out when I reach it."

"I agree," said Bear. "Tomorrow we will race."

When the next day came, many of the other animals had gathered to watch. They lined the banks of the great pond and watched Bear as he rolled in the snow and jumped up and down making himself ready.

Finally, just as the sun was a hand's width in the sky, Turtle's head popped out of the hole in the ice at the starting line. "Bear," he called, "I am ready."

Bear walked quickly to the starting place and as soon as the signal was given, he rushed forward, snow flying from his feet and his breath making great white clouds above his head. Turtle's head disappeared in the first hole and then in almost no time at all reappeared from the next hole, far ahead of Bear.

"Here I am, Bear," Turtle called. "Catch up to me!" And then he was gone again. Bear was **astonished** and ran even faster. But before he could reach the next hole, he saw Turtle's green head pop out of it.

"Here I am, Bear," Turtle called again. "Catch up to me!" Now Bear began to run in earnest. His sides were puffing in and out as he ran and his eyes were becoming

**astonished:** greatly surprised

**bloodshot**, but it was no use. Each time, long before he would reach each of the holes, the ugly green head of Turtle would be there ahead of him, calling out to him to catch up!

**bloodshot:** red

When Bear finally reached the finish line, he was barely able to crawl. Turtle was waiting there for him, surrounded by all the other animals. Bear had lost the race. He dragged himself home in disgrace, so tired that he fell asleep as soon as he reached his home. He was so tired that he slept until the warm breath of the Spring came to the woods again.

It was not long after Bear and all the other animals had left the pond that Turtle tapped on the ice with one long claw. At his signal a dozen ugly heads just like his popped up from the holes all along the edge of the pond. It was Turtle's cousins and brothers, all of whom looked just like him!

"My relatives," Turtle said, "I wish to thank you. Today we have shown Bear that it does not pay to call other people names. We have taught him a good lesson."

Turtle smiled and a dozen other turtles, all just like him, smiled back. "And we have shown the other animals," Turtle said, "That Turtles are not the slowest of the animals."

*Sometimes the word* swift *is used to mean "quick-thinking." In that sense the turtles certainly were swifter than Bear. In your view was Turtle's trick justified? Why or why not? What does this story tell you about the importance of teamwork to the Iroquois?*

Source: Joseph Bruchac, *Turkey Brother, and Other Tales.* New York: The Crossing Press, 1975.

# Paul Revere's Ride

## by Henry Wadsworth Longfellow

*"Paul Revere's Ride" is one of the most famous poems about our country's history. It was published by Henry Wadsworth Longfellow in 1863, in the middle of the Civil War. The poem looks back to the beginning of an earlier war—the American Revolution. It celebrates the night that the silversmith Paul Revere and two other men rode through the countryside to Concord, Massachussets, to warn the American Patriots that the British were about to attack. Thanks to the warning, the colonists were able to prepare for battle. This selection from Longfellow's even longer poem captures the danger and excitement of Revere's mission. Read the poem slowly and try to tell in your own words what is happening in each section.*

Listen, my children, and you shall hear
Of the midnight ride of Paul Revere,
On the eighteenth of April, in Seventy-five;
Hardly a man is now alive
Who remembers that famous day and year.

**He** said to his friend, "If the British march
By land or sea from the town tonight,
Hang a lantern **aloft** in the **belfry** arch
Of the North Church tower as a signal light,—
One, if by land, and two, if by sea;
And I on the opposite shore will be,
Ready to ride and spread the alarm
Through every **Middlesex** village and farm,
For the country folk to be up and to **arm**."

**He:** Paul Revere

**aloft:** high up
**belfry:** a tower where
bells are hung

**Middlesex:** county north
of Boston
**arm:** take up weapons

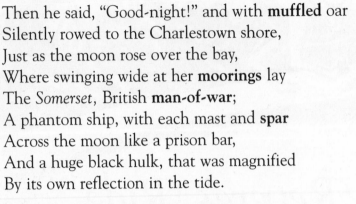

Then he said, "Good-night!" and with **muffled** oar
Silently rowed to the Charlestown shore,
Just as the moon rose over the bay,
Where swinging wide at her **moorings** lay
The *Somerset*, British **man-of-war**;
A phantom ship, with each mast and **spar**
Across the moon like a prison bar,
And a huge black hulk, that was magnified
By its own reflection in the tide.

Meanwhile, **his friend**, through alley and street,
Wanders and watches with eager ears.
Till in the silence around him he hears
The **muster** of men at the **barrack** door,
The sound of arms, and the tramp of feet,
And the measured tread of the **grenadiers**,
Marching down to their boats on the shore.

Then he climbed the tower of the Old North Church,
By the wooden stairs, with **stealthy** tread,
To the belfry-chamber overhead,
And startled the pigeons from their perch
On the **sombre** rafters, that round him made
Masses and moving shapes of shade,—
By the trembling ladder, steep and tall,
To the highest window in the wall,
Where he paused to listen and look down
A moment on the roofs of the town,
And the moonlight flowing over all.

…A moment only he feels the spell
Of the place and the hour, and the secret dread
Of the lonely belfry and **the dead**;
For suddenly all his thoughts are bent
On a shadowy something far away,
Where the river widens to meet the bay,—
A line of black that bends and floats
On the rising tide, like a bridge of boats.

**muffled:** wrapped in something to soften the sound

**moorings:** ropes and anchors
**man-of-war:** armed ship
**spar:** pole

**his friend:** the one who is to send signal with lights

**muster:** gathering
**barrack:** housing for soldiers
**grenadiers:** soldiers

**stealthy:** secretive

**sombre:** dark and gloomy

**the dead:** in church cemetery

Meanwhile, impatient to mount and ride,
Booted and **spurred**, with a heavy stride
On the opposite shore walked Paul Revere.
Now he patted his horse's side,
Now gazed at the landscape far and near,
Then, **impetuous**, stamped the earth,
And turned and tightened his **saddle-girth**;
But mostly he watched with eager search
The belfry-tower of the Old North Church,
As it rose above the graves on the hill,
Lonely and **spectral** and sombre and still.
And **lo!** as he looks, on the belfry's height
A glimmer, and then a gleam of light!
He springs to the saddle, the **bridle** he turns,
But **lingers** and gazes, till full on his sight
A second lamp in the belfry burns!

A hurry of hoofs in a village street,
A shape in the moonlight, a bulk in the dark,
And beneath, from the pebbles, in passing a spark
Struck out by a **steed** flying fearless and **fleet**:
That was all! And yet, through the gloom and the light,
The fate of a nation was riding that night;
And the spark struck out by that steed in his flight,
Kindled the land into flame with its heat. . . .

It was twelve by the village clock,
When he crossed the bridge into Medford town.
He heard the crowing of the cock,
And the barking of the farmer's dog,
And felt the damp of the river fog
That rises after the sun goes down.

It was one by the village clock,
When he galloped into Lexington.
He saw the **gilded weathercock**
Swim in the moonlight as he passed,
And the meeting-house windows, blank and bare,
Gaze at him with a spectral glare,
As if they already stood **aghast**
At the bloody work they would look upon.

**spurred:** wearing spurs to urge horse forward

**impetuous:** suddenly, energetically
**saddle-girth:** strap used to hold saddle in place

**spectral:** ghostly
**lo!:** Look!

**bridle:** horse's reins
**lingers:** stays

**steed:** horse
**fleet:** fast

**gilded weathercock:** gold-coated weather vane

**aghast:** filled with horror

It was two by the village clock,
When he came to the bridge in Concord town.
He heard the **bleating of the flock**,
And the twitter of birds among the trees,
And felt the breath of the morning breeze
Blowing over the meadows brown.
And one was safe and asleep in his bed
Who at the bridge would be first to fall,
Who that day would be lying dead,
Pierced by a British **musket-ball**.

You know the rest. In the books you have read,
How the British Regulars fired and fled,—
How the farmers gave them ball for ball,
From behind each fence and farm-yard wall,
Chasing the red-coats down the lane,
Then crossing the fields to emerge again
Under the trees at the turn of the road,
And only pausing to fire and load.

So through the night rode Paul Revere;
And so through the night went his cry of alarm
To every Middlesex village and farm,—
A cry of **defiance** and not of fear,
A voice in the darkness, a knock at the door,
And a word that shall echo forevermore!
For, **borne** on the night-wind of the Past,
Through all our history, to the last,
In the hour of darkness and **peril** and need,
The people will waken and listen to hear
The hurrying hoof-beats of that steed,
And the midnight message of Paul Revere.

**bleating of the flock:** crying of sheep

**musket-ball:** bullet

**defiance:** bold opposition

**borne:** carried

**peril:** danger

*The Old North Church in Boston, in whose tower the two famous lanterns were hung, still stands. Outside it now stands a statue of Paul Revere. Why do you think Longfellow admired Paul Revere's ride? What message do you think he might have wanted his poem to carry to the people of his own day, in the midst of the Civil War?*

Source: Henry Wadsworth Longfellow, "Paul Revere's Ride," *Anthology of American Poetry*. New York: Crown Publishers, Inc., 1983.

# Hard Times at Valley Forge

**by Joseph Martin, 1777-1778**

*Supplies often ran low during the American Revolution. When General George Washington's army marched to Valley Forge, Pennsylvania, in December 1777, soldiers had little food, clothing, or medicine. One of the soldiers in Washington's army was Joseph Martin, a 17-year-old boy from Milford, Connecticut. Martin kept a diary of those hard times. How do you think people survive such hardships?*

The army was now not only starved but naked. The **greatest part** were not only shirtless and barefoot, but **destitute** of all other clothing, especially blankets. I **procured** a small piece of raw cowhide and made myself a pair of moccasins, which kept my feet (while they lasted) from the frozen ground, although, as I well remember, the hard edges so **galled** my ankles, while on a march, that it was with much difficulty and pain that I could wear them afterwards; but the only **alternative** I had was to **endure** this inconvenience or to go barefoot, as hundreds of my companions had to, till they might be tracked by their blood upon the rough frozen ground. But hunger, nakedness and sore shins were not the only difficulties we had at that time to **encounter**; we had hard duty to perform and little or no strength to perform it with.

The army... marched for the Valley Forge in order to take up our winter **quarters**. We were now in a truly **forlorn** condition,—no clothing, no **provisions** and as disheartened as need be.... Our **prospect** was indeed **dreary**. In our miserable condition, to go into the wild woods and build us **habitations**...in such a weak, starved and naked condition, was appalling in the highest

**greatest part:** most
**destitute of:** lacking
**procured:** got

**galled:** scraped

**alternative:** choice
**endure:** put up with

**encounter:** deal with

**quarters:** housing
**forlorn:** sad
**provisions:** goods, especially food
**prospect:** situation
**dreary:** gloomy
**habitations:** places to live

degree. . . . However, there was no **remedy**, no alternative but this or **dispersion**. But dispersion, I believe, was not thought of, at least, I did not think of it. We had engaged in the defense of our injured country and were willing, nay, we were determined to **persevere** as long as such hardships were not altogether **intolerable**. . . .

    We arrived at the Valley Forge in the evening [December 18]. It was dark; there was no water to be found and I was **perishing with** thirst. I searched for water till I was weary and came to my tent without finding any. **Fatigue** and thirst, joined with hunger, almost made me desperate. I felt at that instant as if I would have taken **victuals** or drink from the best friend I had on earth by force. I am not writing fiction, all are **sober realities**. Just after I arrived at my tent, two soldiers, whom I did not know, passed by. They had some water in their canteens which they told me they had found a good distance off, but could not direct me to the place as it was very dark. I tried to beg a **draught** of water from them but they... [refused]. At length I persuaded them to sell me a drink for three **pence**, Pennsylvania currency, which was every cent of property I could then call my own, so great was the necessity I was then reduced to.

    I lay here two nights and one day and had not a **morsel** of anything to eat all the time, **save** half of a small pumpkin, which I cooked by placing it upon a rock, the skin side uppermost, and making a fire upon it. By the time it was heat[ed] through I devoured it with as keen an appetite as I should a pie made of it at some other time.

**remedy:** cure
**dispersion:** breaking up of the army

**persevere:** continue
**intolerable:** unbearable

**perishing with:** dying of

**fatigue:** tiredness

**victuals:** food
**sober realities:** hard truths

**draught** [draft]: drink

**pence:** pennies

**morsel:** scrap
**save:** except for

*Nearly 3,000 soldiers died at Valley Forge during the winter of 1777–1778—roughly 30 soldiers a day. If the British had attacked they probably could have won an easy victory over the sick and starving American army. But the British never tried. In February 1778 Baron von Steuben, a German officer, came to Valley Forge and helped train and reorganize the troops. Soon American soldiers were healthy and ready for battle. Joseph Martin grew healthier, too, and served in the army until the war's final day. He then became a schoolteacher and laborer and settled in Prospect, Maine.*

Source: Joseph Martin, *A Narrative of Some of the Adventures, Dangers and Sufferings of a Revolutionary Soldier.* Hallowell, Maine, 1830; reprinted Boston: Little, Brown & Company, 1962.

# In the Year of the Boar and Jackie Robinson

**by Bette Bao Lord**

*Coming to the United States as an immigrant can be a puzzling experience, especially if you are a child. Even saying the Pledge of Allegiance or playing an American game can be confusing for a new immigrant. In Bette Bao Lord's novel, Shirley Temple Wong and her mother come to the United States from China in 1947. Shirley finds herself in a fifth-grade classroom in Brooklyn in New York City, struggling to make sense of baseball, the English language, and American customs. Bette Bao Lord's novel is fiction, but the author was herself an immigrant from China, and she experienced many of the difficulties that immigrants face when they have to get used to a new culture. According to Shirley's teacher, in what ways is Shirley like the baseball hero Jackie Robinson?*

**I**t was almost summer. An eager sun outshone the neon sign atop the Squibb factory even before the first bell **beckoned** students to their homerooms. Now alongside the empty milk crates at Mr. P's, brown paper bags with collars neatly rolled boasted plump strawberries, **crimson** cherries and Chiquita bananas. The cloakroom stood empty. Gone, the sweaters, **slickers** and **galoshes**.

At the second bell, the fifth grade, as always, scrambled to their feet. As always, Tommy O'Brien giggled, and each girl checked her seat to see if she was his victim of the day. Susie Spencer, whose tardiness could set clocks, rushed in, her face long with excuses. Popping a last bubble, Maria Gonzales tucked her gum safely behind an ear while Joseph gave an extra stroke to his hair.

**beckoned:** called

**crimson:** red

**slickers:** plastic raincoats
**galoshes:** rain boots

Finally Mrs. Rappaport cleared her throat, and the room was still. With hands over hearts, the class performed the ritual that ushered in another day at school.

Shirley's voice was lost in the chorus.

"I pledge a lesson to the frog of the United States of America, and to the wee puppet for witches' hands. One Asian, in the **vestibule**, with little tea and just rice for all."

"Class, be seated," said Mrs. Rappaport, looking around to see if anyone was absent.

No one was.

"Any questions on the homework?"

All hands remained on or below the decks, etched with initials, new with splinters, brown with age.

"In that case, any questions on any subject at all?"

Irvie's hand shot up. It was quickly pulled down by Maria, who hated even the sound of the word "spider." Spiders were all Irvie ever asked about, talked about, dreamed about. How many eyes do spiders have? Do spiders eat three meals a day? Where are spiders' ears located?

By now, everyone in the fifth grade knew that spiders come with no, six or eight eyes. That spiders do not have to dine regularly and that some can thrive as long as two years without a bite. That spiders are earless.

Since Irvie was as scared of girls as Maria was of spiders, he sat on his hands, but just in case he changed his mind, Maria's hand went up.

"Yes, Maria?"

"Eh . . . eh, I had a question, but I forgot."

"Was it something we discussed yesterday?"

"Yeah, yeah, that's it."

"Something about air currents or cloud formation, perhaps?"

vestibule: entrance hall

"Yeah. How come I see lightning before I hear thunder?"

"Does anyone recall the answer?"

Tommy jumped in. "That's easy. 'Cause your eyes are in front, and your ears are off to the side." To prove his point, he wiggled his ears, which framed his **disarming** smile like the handles of a fancy soup bowl.

Laughter was his reward.

"The correct answer, Maria," said Mrs. Rappaport, trying not to smile too, "is that light waves travel faster than sound waves."

Shirley raised her hand.

"Yes?"

"Who's the girl Jackie Robinson?"

Laughter returned. This time Shirley did not understand the joke. Was the girl very, very bad? So bad that her name should not be uttered in the presence of a grown-up?

Putting a finger to her lips, Mrs. Rappaport quieted the class. "Shirley, you ask an excellent question. A most **appropriate** one. . . ."

The Chinese blushed, wishing her teacher would stop praising her, or at least not in front of the others. Already, they called her "teacher's dog" or "apple shiner."

"Jackie Robinson," Mrs. Rappaport continued, "is a man, the first Negro to play baseball in the major leagues."

"What is a Negro, Mrs. Rappaport?"

"A Negro is someone who is born with dark skin."

"Like Mabel?"

"Like Mabel and Joey and . . . "

"Maria?"

"No, Maria is not a Negro."

"But Maria is dark. Darker than Joey."

"I see what you mean. Let me try again. A Negro is someone whose **ancestors** originally came from Africa and who has dark skin."

"Then why I'm called Jackie Robinson?"

Mrs. Rappaport looked mystified. "Who calls you Jackie Robinson?"

"Everybody."

"Then I'll have to ask them. Mabel?"

" 'Cause she's **pigeon-toed** and stole home."

The teacher nodded. "Well, Shirley, it seems you are not only a good student, but a good baseball player."

**disarming:** charming

**appropriate:** fitting

**ancestors:** relatives from long ago

**pigeon-toed:** a person whose feet point toward each other

There, she'd done it again! The kids would surely call her "a shiner of apples for teacher's dog" next. Shirley's unhappiness must have been obvious, because Mrs. Rappaport evidently felt the need to explain further.

"It is a compliment, Shirley. Jackie Robinson is a big hero, especially in Brooklyn, because he plays for the Dodgers."

"Who is dodgers?" Shirley asked.

That question, like a **wayward** torch in a roomful of firecrackers, sparked answers from everyone.

**wayward:** stray

"De Bums!"

"The best in the history of baseball!"

"Kings of Ebbets Field!"

"They'll kill the Giants!"

"They'll murder the Yankees!"

"The swellest guys in the world!"

"America's favorites!"

"Winners!"

Mrs. Rappaport clapped her hands for order. The girls quieted down first, followed **reluctantly** by the boys. That's better. Participation is welcome, but one at a time. Let's do talk about baseball!"

**reluctantly:** without wanting to

"Yay!" shouted the class.

"And let's combine it with **civics** too!"

**civics:** citizenship

The class did not welcome this proposal as eagerly, but Mrs. Rappaport went ahead anyway.

"Mabel, tell us why baseball is America's favorite **pastime**."

Pursing her lips in disgust at so ridiculous a question, Mabel answered. " 'Cause it's a great game. Everybody plays it, loves it and follows the games on the radio and **nabs** every chance to go and see it."

"True," said Mrs. Rappaport, nodding. "But what is it about baseball that is ideally suited to Americans?"

Mabel turned around, looking for an answer from someone else, but **to no avail**. There was nothing to do but throw the question back. "Whatta ya mean by 'suits'?"

"I mean, is there something special about baseball that fits the special kind of people we are and the special kind of country America is?" Mrs. Rappaport tilted her head to one side, inviting a response. When none came, she sighed a sigh so **fraught with** disappointment that it sounded as if her heart were breaking.

No one wished to be a party to such a sad event, so everybody found some urgent business to attend to like scratching, slumping, sniffing, scribbling, squinting, sucking teeth or removing dirt from underneath a fingernail. Joseph cracked his knuckles.

The ticking of the big clock became so loud that President Washington and President Lincoln, who occupied the wall space to either side of it, exchanged a look of shared displeasure.

But within the frail, birdlike body of Mrs. Rappaport was the spirit of a dragon capable of tackling the heavens and earth. With a quick toss of her red hair, she proceeded to answer her own question with such feeling that no one who heard could be so unkind as to ever forget. Least of all Shirley.

"Baseball is not just another sport. America is not just another country. . . . "

If Shirley did not understand every word, she took its meaning to heart. Unlike Grandfather's stories which quieted the warring spirits within her with the softness of moonlight or the **lyric timbre** of a lone flute, Mrs. Rappaport's speech thrilled her like sunlight and trumpets.

"In our national pastime, each player is a member of a team, but when he comes to bat, he stands alone. One man. Many opportunities. For no matter how far behind, how late in the game, he, by himself, can make a difference. He can change what has been. He can make it a new ball game.

**pastime:** hobby

**nabs:** grabs

**to no avail:** with no luck

**fraught with:** full of

**lyric timbre:** tone

73

"In the life of our nation, each man is a citizen of the United States, but he has the right to pursue his own happiness. For no matter what his race, religion or creed, be he **pauper** or president, he has the right to speak his mind, to live as he wishes within the law, to elect our officials and stand for office, to **excel**. To make a difference. To change what has been. To make a better America.

"And so can you! And so must you!"

Shirley felt as if the walls of the classroom had vanished. **In their stead** was a frontier of doors to which she held the keys.

"This year, Jackie Robinson is at bat. He stands for himself, for Americans of every **hue**, for an America that honors fair play.

"Jackie Robinson is the grandson of a slave, the son of a **sharecropper**, raised in poverty by a lone mother who took in ironing and washing. But a woman determined to achieve a better life for her son. And she did. For despite **hostility** and **injustice**, Jackie Robinson went to college, excelled in all sports, served his country in war. And now, Jackie Robinson is at bat in the big leagues. Jackie Robinson is making a difference. Jackie Robinson has changed what has been. And Jackie Robinson is making a better America.

"And so can you! And so must you!"

Suddenly Shirley understood why her father had brought her ten thousand miles to live among strangers. Here, she did not have to wait for gray hairs to be considered wise. Here, she could speak up, question even the conduct of the President. Here, Shirley Temple Wong was somebody. She felt as if she had the power of ten tigers, as if she had grown as tall as the Statue of Liberty.

**pauper:** poor person

**excel:** do very well

**in their stead:** in their place

**hue:** color

**sharecropper:** a farmer who rents land by paying a share of the crop raised on the land

**hostility:** anger
**injustice:** unfair ways

*Shirley learns to speak English fluently and makes friends with her American classmates. They are all delighted when Jackie Robinson wins the "Rookie of the Year" award and the Dodgers win the National League pennant. You can read the novel to find out how Shirley actually meets her hero, Jackie Robinson.*

Source: Bette Bao Lord, *In the Year of the Boar and Jackie Robinson.* New York: Harper & Row, 1984.

# I Was Dreaming To Come To America
## Memories from the Ellis Island Oral History Project

**selected by Veronica Lawlor**

*The early years of the twentieth century brought millions of immigrants to the United States. Many of the immigrants passed through Ellis Island. These interview excerpts are from the book I Was Dreaming to Come to America, which grew out of the Ellis Island Oral History Project. Oral history is a historical account obtained by recording interviews with people who can give firsthand descriptions of past events. For the Ellis Island project, people were interviewed about their experiences in coming to America. Why did so many people leave their homes to come to this country?*

"...Going to America then was almost like going to the moon.... We were all bound for places about which we knew nothing at all and for a country that was totally strange to us."

> Golda Meir
> Russia
> Arrived in 1906 • Age 8

"Coming to America had meaning. I was a kid of seven and in contrast to what I had gone through, Ellis Island was like not a **haven**, but a heaven. I don't remember any fright when I got to Ellis Island.

"My father's dream and prayer always was 'I must get my family to America.'... America was paradise, the streets

**haven:** place of safety

were covered with gold. And when we arrived here, and when we landed from Ellis Island and [went] to Buffalo, it was as if God's great promise had been fulfilled that we would eventually find freedom."

Vartan Hartunian
Turkey (Armenian)
Arrived in 1922 • Age 7

"My first impressions of the new world will always remain etched in my memory, particularly that hazy October morning when I first saw Ellis Island. The steamer *Florida*, 14 days out of Naples, filled to capacity with 1,600 natives of Italy, had weathered one of the worst storms in our captain's memory. Glad we were, both children and grown-ups, to leave the open sea and come at last through the narrows into the bay.

"My mother, my stepfather, my brother Giuseppe, and my two sisters, Liberta and Helvetia, all of us together, happy that we had come through the storm safely, clustered on the **foredeck** for fear of separation and looked with wonder on this miraculous land of our dreams."

**foredeck:** forward part of ship's main deck

Edward Corsi
Italy
Arrived in 1907 • Age 10

"Most dear to me are the shoes my mother wore when she first set foot on the soil of America. . . . She landed in America in those shoes and somehow or the other she felt that she was going to hang on to them. They are brown high-top shoes that had been soled and resoled and stitched and mended in Sweden to hold then together till she could get to America. We just kept them. And then . . . as I grew up and everything, I said, 'Don't ever throw them away'."

Birgitta Hedman Fichter
Sweden
Arrived in 1924 • Age 6

"I feel like I had two lives. You plant something in the ground, it has its roots, and then you **transplant** it where it stays permanently. That's what happened to me. You put an end . . . and forget about your childhood; I became a man here. All of a sudden, I started life new, amongst people whose language I didn't understand. . . . [It was a] different life; everything was different. . . but I never **despaired**, I was optimistic.

**transplant:** move from one place to another

"And this is the only country where you're not a stranger, because we are all strangers. It's only a matter of time who got here first."

**despaired:** gave up hope

Lazarus Salamon
Hungary
Arrived in 1920 • Age 16

"When I was about 10 years old I said, 'I have to go to America.' Because my uncles were here already, and it kind of got me that I want to go to America, too. . . . I was dreaming about it. I was writing to my uncles, I said I wish one day I'll be in America. I was dreaming to come to America. . . . And I was dreaming, and my dream came true. When I came here, I was in a different world. It was so peaceful. It was quiet. You were not afraid to go out in the middle of the night. . . . I'm free. I'm just like a bird. You can fly and land on any tree and you're free."

Helen Cohen
Poland
Arrived in 1920 • Age 20

*What did the immigrants interviewed have in common? What do you think made them so optimistic about life in the United States? If you were helping to record the oral history of these people, what questions would you ask them?*

Source: Veronica Lawlor, ed., *I Was Dreaming to Come to America: Memories from the Ellis Island Oral History Project.* New York: Penguin Books USA Inc., 1995.

# City, City

**by Marci Ridlon**

*If you have ever lived in a city, you know that there are both good sides and bad sides to living there. In the poem below, how does Marci Ridlon express both the good sides and bad sides of urban life?*

**I**

City, city,

Wrong and bad,

**Looms** above me

When I'm sad,

Throws its shadow

On my care,

Sheds its poison

In my air,

Pounds me with its

Noisy fist,

Sprays me with its

**Sooty** mist.

Till, with sadness

On my face,

I long to live

Another place.

**II**

City, city,

**Golden-clad,**

Shines around me

When I'm glad,

Lifts me with its

Strength and height,

Fills me with its

Sound and sight,

Takes me to its

Crowded heart,

Holds me so I

Won't depart.

Till, with gladness

On my face,

I wouldn't live

Another place.

**golden-clad:** dressed in gold

**looms:** towers

**sooty:** covered with ashes

*What do you like about the type of community you live in? What do you dislike? You might like to write a two-part poem about the good sides and bad sides of living in a rural or suburban neighborhood.*

Source: Marci Ridlon, *That Was Summer.* New York: Follett Publishing Company, 1969.

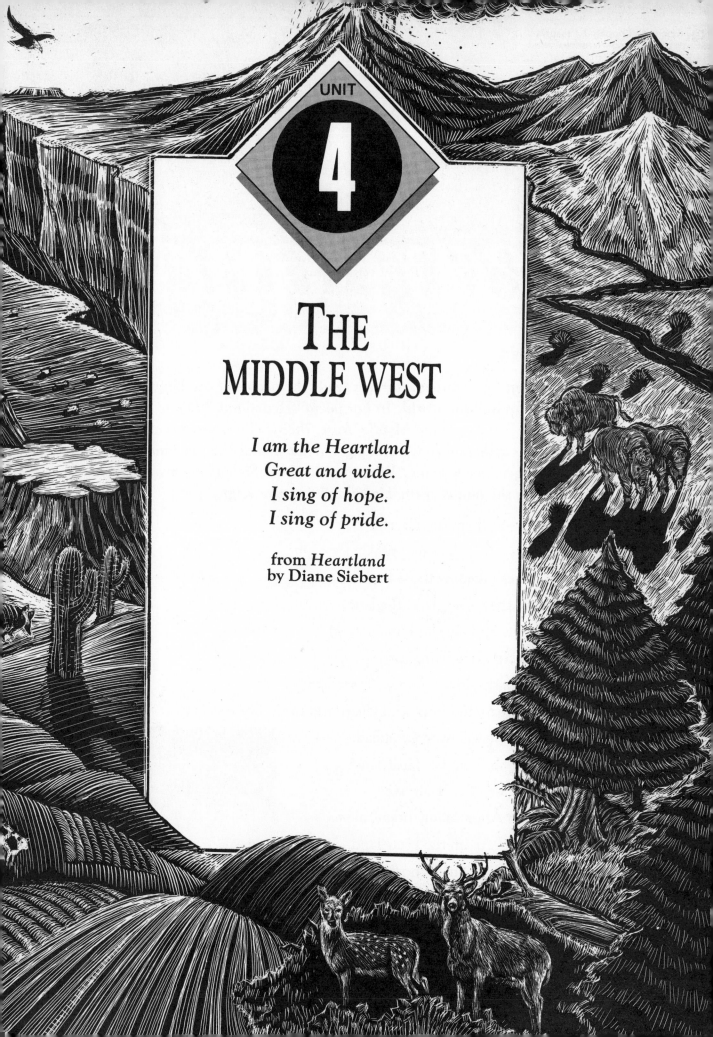

# THE MIDDLE WEST

*I am the Heartland
Great and wide.
I sing of hope.
I sing of pride.*

from *Heartland*
by Diane Siebert

# Heartland

**by Diane Siebert**

*The food grown by American farmers feeds the people of the United States and many people around the world. In her poem "Heartland," Diane Siebert celebrates the farmers of the Middle West, their fields of corn and wheat, and their herds of cattle and sheep and pigs. What makes the flat land of the Middle West good for farming? What do you think Siebert means when she writes that on the plains of the Heartland "nature reigns"?*

I am the Heartland.

Hear me speak

In voices raised by those who seek

To live their lives upon the land,

To know and love and understand

The secrets of a living earth—

Its strengths, its weaknesses, its worth;

Who, Heartland born and Heartland **bred,**     **bred: raised**

Possess the will to move ahead.

I am the Heartland.

I survive

To keep America, my home, alive.

I am the Heartland.

Smell the fields,

The rich, dark earth, and all it yields;

The air before a coming storm,

80

A newborn calf, so damp and warm;
The dusty grain in barns that hold
The bales of hay, all green and gold.

For I have learned of drought and hail,
Of floods and frosts and crops that fail,
And of tornadoes as they move . . .

In frightening paths, again to prove
That in the Heartland, on these plains,
Despite Man's power, Nature **reigns**.

reigns: rules

Before me, summer stretches out
With pastures **draped** in **lush**, green grass,
And as the days of growing pass,

draped: covered
lush: thick

I feel the joy when fields of grain
Are blessed by sunlight, warmth, and rain;
And winter, white and cold, **descends**

descends: falls

With blizzards howling as they sweep
Across me, piling snowdrifts deep.
Then days grow longer, skies turn clear,
And all the gifts of spring appear—
The young are born, the **seedlings** sprout;

seedlings: young
green plants

     I am the Heartland:

       Earth and sky
And changing seasons passing by.
I feel the touch of autumn's chill,
And as its colors brightly spill

Across the land, the growing ends,
       I am the Heartland.

       In my song
Are cities beating, steady, strong,
With footsteps from a million feet
And sounds of traffic in the street;
Where giant mills and stockyards **sprawl**,

sprawl: stretch out

And neon-lighted shadows fall
From windowed walls of brick that rise

Toward the clouds, to scrape the skies;

Where highways meet and rails **converge**;

converge: come together to one point

Where farm and city rhythms **merge**

merge: blend, join

To form a **vital** bond between

vital: very important

The concrete and the fields of green.

I am the Heartland.

On these plains

Rise elevators filled with grains.

They mark the towns where people walk

To see their neighbors, just to talk;

Where farmers go to get supplies

And sit a spell to **analyze**

analyze: think about

The going price of corn and beans,

The rising cost of new machines;

Where steps are meant for shelling peas,

And kids build houses in the trees.

I am the Heartland.

On this soil

Live those who through the seasons **toil**:

toil: work

The farmer, with his spirit strong;

The farmer, working hard and long,

A feed-and-seed-store cap in place,

Pulled down to shield a weathered face—

A face whose every crease and line

Can tell a tale, and help define

A lifetime spent beneath the sun,

A life of work that's never done.

By miles of wood and wire stretched

Around the barns and pastures where

The smell of **livestock** fills the air.

livestock: farm animals

These are the farms where hogs are bred,

The farms where chicks are hatched and fed;

The farms where dairy cows are raised,

The farms where cattle herds are grazed;

The farms with horses, farms with sheep—
Upon myself, all these I keep.
A patchwork quilt laid gently down
In hues of yellow, green, and brown
As tractors, plows, and planters go
Across my fields and, row by row,
Prepare the earth and plant the seeds
That grow to meet a nation's needs.

       I am the Heartland.
        I can feel
Machines of iron, tools of steel,
Creating farmlands, square by square—
A quilt of life I proudly wear:
       I am the Heartland.
        Shaped and lined
By rivers, great and small, that wind
Past farms, whose barns and silos stand
Like treasures in my fertile hand.
       I am the Heartland.
        Great and wide.
        I sing of hope.
        I sing of pride.
I am the land where wheat fields grow
In golden waves that **ebb and flow**;
Where cornfields stretched across the plains
Lie green between the country lanes.

**ebb and flow:** come in
and out with the
tides

*The Middle West has some of the darkest, richest soil in the world. The region has sometimes been called the Corn Belt and sometimes the Breadbasket. Why do you think Diane Siebert calls it the Heartland?*

Source: Diane Siebert, *Heartland*. New York: Thomas Y. Crowell, 1989.

# Skylark

### by Patricia MacLachlan

*In* Skylark, *Patricia MacLachlan continues the story of Sarah Wheaton and the Witting family, which she began in the book* Sarah, Plain and Tall. *Sarah has come from Maine to the Middle West in response to Jacob Witting's advertisement for a wife. She has grown close to Jacob and to his children, Caleb and Anna, but the climate of the Middle West is still strange to her. In this excerpt from the novel, Anna tells of a terrible drought that dries up the wells and streams, threatening the lives of farm families. Feeling angry and helpless, Sarah distances herself from the land, where she has not yet made a real home. What does her neighbor Maggie mean when she says, "You have to write your name in the land to live here"?*

My dreams are cool. They are cool and the color of the sky before rain, a dark and peaceful blue, the clouds edged in black before the rain comes and the earth smells sharp and sweet. I remember that smell.

The days are hot and still now.

Only my dreams are cool.

We sat on the porch out of the terrible sun, Maggie fanning herself, Sarah mixing batter for biscuits. **Rose** and **Violet** rolled a ball in the dirt to **Tom**. Caleb sat watching the sky for clouds.

**Rose, Violet, Tom:** Maggie's children

"This heat," said Maggie wearily. "I dream of my old home sometimes. And I dream of long, cool mornings of sleep without the baby waking!"

Sarah smiled.

"Night dreams or daydreams?" she asked.

"What's a day dream?" asked Caleb.

Sarah sat back and looked at Tom crawling happily in the dirt.

"Sometimes, no matter where you are, you think of something sweet and cool. A place, maybe. And suddenly it's there. Or maybe it's something you wish for . . . and it is so near you can touch it, smell it . . . hear the sound of it . . ."

Sarah looked up suddenly as if caught up in her thoughts.

"She's dreaming about Maine," Caleb whispered to me.

*No. It's not Maine,* I thought. *It's not Maine she's thinking about. It's something else.*

Tom grabbed the ball and held it over his head. Sarah smiled.

"I have dreams, Sarah," Caleb said.

"Good dreams, Caleb?" she asked.

"I dream about rain," said Caleb. "Do you? Do you dream about rain?"

Sarah reached over and took Caleb on her lap.

"Yes, Caleb. I dream about rain."

"Good," he said. "Then it will come true."

But rain was only in our dreams. The winds came every day, blowing dust through the windows and into the house until it covered the furniture and got into the food and our clothes and hair. The land got even drier, and we stopped taking baths. Every day we hauled river water for the animals in big wooden barrels.

And then the worst thing happened.

We drove to the river in our wagon, empty barrels in the back. Clouds hung high in the sky. Maggie sat in her wagon by the riverbed. **Matthew** stood on the bluff over the river, looking down.

**Matthew:** Maggie's husband

"Hello, Maggie," called Sarah.

But Maggie didn't speak. She didn't even look at us.

We got down from the wagon. The river was nearly dry, only a small trickle in the red prairie dirt.

Everyone was quiet.

"What will we do?" whispered Sarah.

"We'll have to travel farther for water," said Papa.

"Think about it, Jacob," said Matthew. "It will be a three-day trip, maybe four. When we get back home, then what? Water for the crops? There *are* no crops."

Papa looked at Matthew, then away over the land.

Matthew sighed.

"Maggie and I have been talking about another way," he said.

"What?" asked Sarah.

"I think that what Matthew means is that they're thinking about leaving," said Papa softly.

Sarah turned and looked up at Maggie in the wagon.

"Leaving?" she said, her voice rough and dry like the fields.

Maggie climbed down and went behind the wagon, Sarah following her. I walked closer and stood out of sight, and saw Sarah put out her hand to touch Maggie. But Maggie took a step away, as if Sarah's comfort was too hard. And I heard words I wish I hadn't heard.

"I hate this land," said Sarah. "I don't have to love it the way Matthew and Jacob love it. They give it everything. Everything! And it gives nothing back."

"They don't know anywhere else, Sarah," said Maggie.

I closed my eyes, but I couldn't close out Sarah's words.

"Jacob once said his name was written in this land, but mine isn't. It isn't!" said Sarah angrily.

"You are like the prairie lark, you know," said Maggie. "It sings its song above the land to let all the birds know it's there before it plunges down to earth to make its home. But you have not come to earth, Sarah."

There was silence then, and I opened my eyes again.

"You don't have to love this land," said Maggie. "But if you don't love it, you won't survive. Jacob's right. You have to write your name in the land to live here."

Sarah didn't speak. She took a handful of dry prairie grass in her hands, letting it crumble through her fingers. Then she walked away from us, through the dried grass, out onto the brown prairie that stretched all the way to the sky. She stood there all alone until Papa went to tell her it was time to go home.

*Later in the novel, Sarah must go back to Maine with the Witting children to wait for the drought to end. The children are excited to see the ocean for the first time, but they all—including Sarah—miss their home in the Middle West. Before too long, however, it rains on the prairie, and they are able to return home. When they arrive, Sarah picks up a stick—and writes her name in the dirt. Although, as in this story, the summer on the prairie can be very hot, winter can be bitterly cold. What causes the extremes of temperature in the Middle West? What are the benefits of the region's climate?*

Source: Patricia MacLachlan, *Skylark*. New York: HarperCollins, 1994.

# LIFE ON THE PRAIRIE

*Laura Ingalls Wilder grew up on the prairie in the late 1800s. She later wrote eight books about her childhood adventures. Millions of people have grown up reading and loving the stories about the "little house on the prairie." Through her books, readers feel they have gotten to know the Ingalls family. Below are some pictures from Laura Ingalls Wilder's life. What do they show you about life on the prairie in the late 1800s?*

In the first winter that the Ingalls family spent in De Smet, Minnesota, they were hit by a major blizzard. Sixty years later, Laura wrote a novel about that winter. She wrote in pencil on school paper. The first page of The Hard Winter is shown at left.

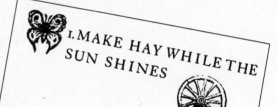

## I. MAKE HAY WHILE THE SUN SHINES

THE MOWING machine's whirring sounded cheerfully from the old buffalo wallow south of the claim shanty, where bluestem grass stood thick and tall and Pa was cutting it for hay.

The sky was high and quivering with heat over the shimmering prairie. Half-way down to sunset, the sun blazed as hotly as at noon. The wind was scorching hot. But Pa had hours of mowing yet to do before he could stop for the night.

Laura drew up a pailful of water from the well at the edge of the Big Slough. She rinsed the brown jug till it was cool to her hand. Then she filled it with the fresh, cool water, corked it tightly, and started with it to the hayfield.

Swarms of little white butterflies hovered over the path. A dragon-fly with gauzy wings swiftly chased a

Even famous writers have to work hard on every word they write. Laura's novel was later published, but the title was changed to The Long Winter. What similarities and differences can you see between the handwritten page and the words in the printed book?

During "the long winter," Laura (right) and her sisters and her parents huddled around the stove in their little house, trying to keep warm. The photograph at right shows Laura and her sisters the year of that "hard winter."

The Youth's Companion *was a much-loved children's magazine of short stories. Delivery of the magazine was stopped during bad weather. During "the long winter," Laura and her family read the old issues slowly to make them last until the next delivery.*

**Magazines such as** The Youth's Companion **helped to cheer the long, cold nights on the prairies. What are some other activities people do to pass the time during very cold weather? What are some choices available to people of the Middle West today that were not available to Laura and her family?**

# A Boy Named
# ABE
## by Susan Nanus

*Abraham Lincoln, the sixteenth President of the United States, was born in a log cabin in the woods of Kentucky. When he was seven his family moved to Indiana. Always an eager student, young Abe loved to spend his time reading. Later in life he became a lawyer. He served a term in Congress and was elected President in 1860. The Civil War was fought during Lincoln's term of office, and he had the difficult job of seeing our country through the bloodiest period in its history. The play A Boy Named Abe shows the kind of strengths the young Lincoln had as a child. Which of these qualities do you think helped him to become a leader?*

## CAST OF CHARACTERS
**Sally Lincoln,** *Abe's older sister and story narrator*
**Abe Lincoln,** *now in his teens*
**Tom Lincoln,** *Abe's father*
**Nathaniel Brown,** *a wealthy neighbor*
**Josiah Crawford,** *a farmer*
**Mrs. Crawford,** *a farmer*
**Dennis Hanks,** *Abe's cousin*
**James Taylor,** *a storekeeper*

**Mrs. Taylor,** *a storekeeper*
**Gentleman**
**John Dill,** *a ferryman*
**Martha Dill,** *John's wife and partner in the ferry business*
**Squire Samuel Pate,** *a justice of the peace*

**Time:** *the 1820s*
**Setting:** *Pigeon Creek, Indiana*

*The almost-bare stage divides into two sections: indoor scenes, stage right; outdoor scenes, stage left. Signs can be set up on chairs to indicate the different locations.*

*Abe is sitting cross-legged in the woods, reading.*

**Sally:** *(enters downstage right and addresses the audience)* Our play, which is mainly about my brother, Abe, begins in the woods by our cabin.

*Tom Lincoln enters.*

**Tom:** *(calling out)* Abe! Abe Lincoln, where are you?

**Sally:** *(to the audience)* That's my brother Abe over there reading. He's always getting in trouble because he loves books so much.

**Tom:** *(finding Abe reading)* There are a hundred things to do, and I won't have you wasting time!

*Nathaniel Brown, a well-dressed man, enters stage left.*

**Nathaniel:** Tom Lincoln?

**Tom:** Mr. Brown, what are you doing here?

**Nathaniel:** Your wife said I could find you out here in the woods. *(He pulls out a paper from his coat.)* I have the deed right here.

**Abe:** Deed?

**Tom:** Mr. Brown is going to buy some land behind the cabin. Eighteen acres to be exact. Right, Mr. Brown?

**Nathaniel:** That's right, Tom. Now, I brought a pen and some ink, so if you'll just sign your name.... (*He pulls out a quill pen and a little bottle of ink.*)

**Abe:** Uh, Pa—would you like me to read the deed?

**Nathaniel:** There's no need for you to read it. Everything is in perfect order.

**Abe:** You shouldn't sign something without knowing what's in it, Pa.

**Tom:** Hmm. You may be right. Okay. Take a look.

*Tom hands the deed to Abe, who begins to read. Tom leans to look at the deed. Nathaniel Brown sneaks away, stage left.*

**Abe:** Just what I thought.

**Tom:** What?

**Abe:** If you sign this, Pa, he'll get the whole farm.

**Tom:** What! You mean he tried to cheat me? Why, you . . . (*He looks around, sees that Nathaniel is gone.*) Well, Abe, looks like for once your reading came in pretty handy.

**Sally:** After that, Pa doesn't bother Abe so much about his reading. A couple of years go by. Abe is the tallest, strongest boy in Pigeon Creek. Now other folks pay to have him work on their farms. This is what happens in the Crawfords' kitchen.

*The Crawfords enter. Josiah has an account book and pen. Mrs. Crawford begins to make an apple pie. Abe enters stage right.*

**Josiah:** Well, Abe, you've been both a farmhand and carpenter this week. You plowed and planted the back field, repaired the barn roof, and built a new fence. I guess I owe you a pretty penny for all that.

**Abe:** Yes, Sir.

**Mrs. Crawford:** If you'll wait a while, I'll have some fresh-baked apple pie for you.

**Abe:** Thanks, Mrs. Crawford, but I better get home. Only...

**Josiah:** Well, what is it, boy? Speak up.

**Abe:** I was wondering...if you don't mind...if I could maybe borrow one of those books? (*He points to an imaginary bookshelf.*)

**Josiah:** You hear that, Mrs. Crawford? Abe prefers a book to a piece of your pie!

**Abe:** Oh, I'm sorry, I didn't mean ...

**Mrs. Crawford:** Nonsense, Abe. I know what you meant. And you just help yourself to any book on that shelf.

**Abe:** Thank you! (*He approaches the shelf and reads the titles.*) I think I'll take *The Life of George Washington* by Mason Weems. (*He takes the book from the shelf gently.*) I really want to study him.

**Josiah:** Abe, with all this studying, you'll go far. Maybe as far as Washington! (*He laughs at his joke.*)

**Mrs. Crawford:** Oh, Josiah! That really wasn't funny!

*The Crawfords exit stage right, as Abe starts reading.*

**Sally:** (*setting up The Lincolns' Cabin sign*) That night, Abe stays up half the night, reading his new book.

*As Sally speaks, Abe closes the book and puts it in a crack in the wall between two imaginary logs. Then Abe gets into bed and falls asleep.*

**Sally:** Abe sleeps in the loft. There's a big storm. Rain drips through the cracks and ...the book is ruined! Our cousin Dennis finds Abe the next day.

*Dennis enters stage right and walks to Abe.*

**Dennis:** What's the matter? You sick or something?

**Abe:** Look what happened to Mr. Crawford's book! I don't believe it! It's all wet and wrinkled from the rain.

**Dennis:** Oh, boy! You're in for it now. What will you say? The cabin burned down? A robber stole it?

**Abe:** I'd sure like to have an excuse, but I don't. I guess I'll just have to tell Mr. Crawford the truth.

**Dennis:** Old Honest Abe, huh, boy?

**Abe:** I guess so, Dennis.

**Sally:** So Abe goes and tells Mr. Crawford just what happened. (*As she speaks, Josiah Crawford enters.*)

**Josiah:** That book cost a lot of money, Abe.

**Abe:** I know, Sir.

**Josiah:** And money doesn't grow on trees.

**Abe:** I know, Sir.

**Josiah:** Lending you the book was generous on my part.

**Abe:** Indeed it was, Sir.

**Josiah:** It was your responsibility to take good care of it.

**Abe:** (*looking down*) Yes, Sir.

**Josiah:** Well, it was an accident. But you can work off the cost. Three days in the fields should do it.

**Abe:** (*gratefully*) Yes, Sir. And . . . here's the book. (*He holds it out.*) You can still read the pages inside.

**Josiah:** You want it? You can have it. As long as you don't read it on the job. Now, get to work!

**Abe:** Yes, Mr. Crawford. And thank you. Thank you so much!

*Josiah and the others clear the chairs, leaving the table as a store counter. Josiah exits stage right as the Taylors enter and stand on one side of the counter, Abe on the other.*

**Sally:** In 1825, Abe is 16. He helps the Taylors run their store. The store is at Posey's Landing on the bank of Anderson's Creek, close to the Ohio River. Steamboats go up and down the Ohio, and there's a ferry that takes folks from here to the other side of the river, where the boats dock. The Taylors are about to leave on a trip.

**James:** Now remember, Abe. The beans are over there and the flour is in the back.

**Mrs. Taylor:** We don't give credit, remember that.

**Abe:** Yes, Ma'am.

**James:** (*pointing*) Nails and other hardware over here.

**Mrs. Taylor:** No money, no merchandise.

**Abe:** Yes, Mrs. Taylor.

**James:** (*nodding toward an imaginary shelf*) Cloth and dress patterns on the shelf.

**Abe:** You know, it's getting late.

**James:** He's right! Come on, Mrs. Taylor, we've a coach to catch, and the driver doesn't plan to wait for us. (*James takes her arm, and they exit.*)

**Abe:** (*goes to the door and peers in both directions*) No customers in sight, so . . . (*He pulls a book from his pocket and begins to read.*)

*A gentleman rushes into the store.*

**Gentleman:** (*with agitation*) Quick! That rowboat outside. Whose is it?

**Abe:** Well, it's mine, but—

**Gentleman:** I'll give you two dollars to row me out to the steamboat right now.

**Abe:** Well . . . okay. Let's go.

*The two rush stage left to an imaginary rowboat. Abe pantomimes rowing it.*

**Sally:** But what Abe thinks is a good deed almost gets him into trouble.

*The Dills enter stage left and stand on the riverbank, watching as Abe approaches.*

**Sally:** The Dills own the ferry that takes passengers from the shore across the river to where the boats dock.

**John:** (*showing disbelief*) Do you see what I see, Martha?

**Martha:** How dare he! Who is he?

**John:** It's Abe Lincoln. The Pigeon Creek boy who works for the Taylors. He could steal our business, Martha.

*Midstream, the gentleman climbs out of the rowboat and onto the steamboat and exits stage left. Abe starts rowing back to the store.*

**John:** Hey, you! Abe Lincoln!

**Martha:** Come over here a minute, will you?

**Abe:** What for?

*Abe reverses direction and rows toward the Dills.*

**John:** Don't you know you can't ferry people across the river without a license? You've broken the law!

**Martha:** We have a license, and you don't!

**John:** You're coming with us, young man!

**Martha:** If the Justice of the Peace finds you guilty, you'll be thrown in jail!

*Martha takes one of Abe's arms; John takes the other. They half-lead, half-pull him stage right as Squire Samuel Pate, carrying his gavel, enters the courtroom from stage right.*

**Sally:** And that is how Abe comes to meet Squire Samuel Pate, Justice of the Peace, who is holding forth right now.

**Squire Pate:** Order! Order in the court. State your case.

**John:** Your Honor, Martha and I have a license to ferry passengers across the river. And we caught this boy red-handed rowing a man to the steamboat.

**Squire Pate:** *(to Abe)* What do you say to that, young man?

**Abe:** What he says is true. But their license is to carry folks across the river. I only went to the middle. So I don't think I really broke the law.

**Squire Pate:** *(pulling out a thick book and leafing through it)* The law is plain. You two have the right to set a person across, but there's no law against rowing passengers to midstream.

**John:** What! But that's not fair!

**Squire Pate:** *(banging his gavel)* Quiet! Case closed.

*John and Martha storm out stage left.*

**Squire Pate:** You've got a good head on your shoulders, young man. What's your name?

**Abe:** Abraham Lincoln, Sir. I'm interested in the law.

**Squire Pate:** Then you should read this book. Knowing the law of the land never hurts.

*Abe takes the book reverently.*

**Squire Pate:** Would you like to come to my court and listen in sometime?

**Abe:** You would let me do that, Your Honor?

**Squire Pate:** Yes I would. I believe you want to learn. And I'd not be surprised if you want to do something big with what you learn. Am I right?

**Abe:** I hope I can, Sir. I will surely try.

**Squire Pate:** Young man, I expect great things of you.

**Sally:** And that's how Abe took his first step toward being a lawyer and after that a congressman and after that . . . well, you already know. Abe was always determined to learn and to do something good with what he learned. Thank you, Squire Pate, for helping Abe take that first important step.

*There are many stories told about Abraham Lincoln's youth. Some might be true, some might be made up, but all are entertaining. The writer of this play chose a few stories that she had read about Abraham Lincoln and dramatized them—or made them into scenes in a play. If you wanted to do the same, how could you find additional stories about Lincoln's life to dramatize? What kind of story do you think would make a good scene?*

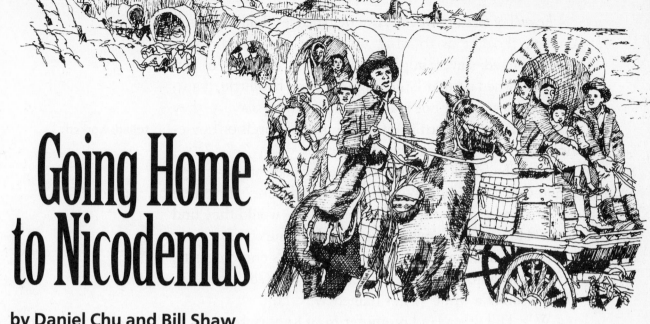

# Going Home to Nicodemus

## by Daniel Chu and Bill Shaw

*Going Home to Nicodemus tells the true story of the town built by African Americans who traveled west to the frontier territory of Kansas after the Civil War. These pioneers, nearly all of them freed slaves, were part of a huge migration, as settlers headed west in search of the free land promised by the Homestead Act of 1862. This selection introduces Nicodemus through the experience of Willianna Hickman and her family, who were among the first settlers in Nicodemus. What did Mrs. Hickman think when she first saw the town? Why do you think she and the others decided to stay?*

The year was 1878, and Willianna Hickman found herself in a place she had never been before. Kansas was its name, and it was, Willianna had been told, the "Promised Land."

Willianna Hickman was thirty-one years old and a woman of color. This was one of the terms commonly used in the nineteenth century to describe an African American. Willianna and her husband, the Reverend Daniel Hickman, had traveled to Kansas from Georgetown, in north central Kentucky where the Reverend Hickman had been the minister of the Mount Olive Baptist Church.

All but the youngest in Daniel's Kentucky **congregation** had been born in slavery. But now, thirteen years after the end of the American Civil War, they were free men and women. No longer could they be bought and sold as property to be kept or **disposed of** at the whim of masters.

**congregation:** church group

**disposed of:** gotten rid of

For all of that, however, America's leaders had not given enough thought as to what was to become of the four million freed slaves in the South. The freed men and women owned neither land nor homes and had little, if any, money. Most could not read or write. During slavery, they had **toiled** on southern plantations as field hands or household servants. They knew little else.

toiled: worked

Now they were at liberty to leave the plantations and go wherever they wished. But where would that be? How were they to feed and house themselves? Where would they find work? How could people who had so little survive?

For the members of Reverend Hickman's church group, an answer came during the winter of 1877–1878. It came in the person of a white visitor named W.R. Hill.

W.R. Hill was a land **promoter** from Kansas, far away to the west. Hill told the Georgetown church members that there was government land available for **homesteading** on the western frontier. There was lots of it, and it was practically free for the asking. To claim a quarter section of land—160 acres—a homesteader had little more to do than show up.

promoter: person who organizes and furthers a business plan

homesteading: claiming and settling on land granted by United States government for farming

Think of it! How could someone who had nothing, and no way of getting anything, turn down an offer like that?

The idea of homesteading became more attractive as Hill talked on. He and his partners had put together a special package for blacks only: a new town on the prairie run by blacks **exclusively** for blacks. Even as he spoke, W.R. Hill confided, hundreds of black settlers already were moving to this new community, a town that bore an **intriguing** name: Nicodemus.

exclusively: only

intriguing: curiousity-arousing

To the Georgetown, Kentucky church audience on that wintry night, W.R. Hill's words were like an answered prayer. Here was a chance, the first for any of them, to own a piece of land, to be independent and self-supporting, to make their own way in life. It was a chance to leave behind the racial **hostility** and discrimination they had always known.

hostility: show of hatred

Out on the open plains of the Kansas frontier, W.R. Hill said, blacks and whites would live as equals.

With the coming of spring, about two hundred members of the Reverend Hickman's church packed up their few belongings and joined the great western **migration**. From the hills of Kentucky, they went off in two groups for Kansas and a new life.

**migration:** movement

The migrants from Kentucky reached Ellis in western Kansas by rail in just a few days. But an outbreak of measles among the children brought sudden tragedy. Some of them died, but Daniel and Willianna Hickman and their six children were among the luckier ones. They survived the outbreak. After a two-week delay in Ellis, the Hickmans and the other families hired horses and wagons for the final leg of their journey.

What a journey it was!

Guided by compass, they traveled two more days across roadless plains marked here and there by a few trees, deer trails, and buffalo wallows, or watering holes. At night the men built roaring campfires and fired their guns in the air to keep wild animals away. The women unpacked bedding and cooked a meal while the children slept or played games within the shadow of the fire's glow.

Worn from travel, Willianna Hickman was almost totally **spent** by the time her group arrived at its destination. She felt even worse when she got her first look at it.

**spent:** exhausted

Nicodemus was not the Promised Land she had expected, not what she had hoped for. To Willianna's **dismay**, there lay before her an entire community of people living in holes in the ground. The people were **burrowed** into the earth like the prairie dogs Willianna had seen on the trek from Ellis.

**dismay:** frightened amazement

**burrowed:** dug

More than a half century later, when she was ninety, Willianna Hickman still **vividly** remembered her shock and astonishment on that spring day in 1878:

**vividly:** clearly

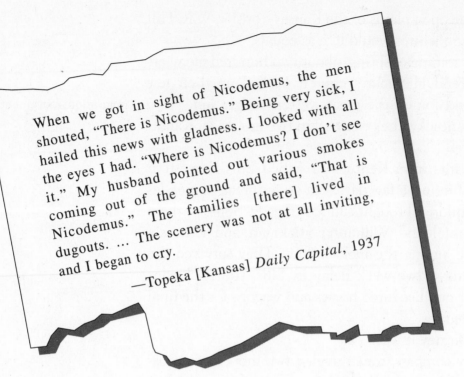

When we got in sight of Nicodemus, the men shouted, "There is Nicodemus." Being very sick, I hailed this news with gladness. I looked with all the eyes I had. "Where is Nicodemus? I don't see it." My husband pointed out various smokes coming out of the ground and said, "That is Nicodemus." The families [there] lived in dugouts. ... The scenery was not at all inviting, and I began to cry.

—Topeka [Kansas] *Daily Capital*, 1937

...Despite her crushing disappointment, Willianna Hickman, her family, and their fellow pioneers did not turn back. The rough conditions of life on the western frontier, in circumstances so lacking in comforts, stunned even those who had experienced the cruelties of slavery. The new hardships they faced were many, more than enough to discourage all but the bravest and strongest.

Most of the pioneers from Kentucky stayed. They **coped** and endured. They held to their hopes and dreams and kept their faith. And because they and their children did what they did, Nicodemus has survived as the oldest—and now the only remaining—all-black frontier town on the Great Plains.

**coped:** struggled successfully

The holes in the ground that greeted Willianna Hickman are long gone now, but Nicodemus is still there.

*What do you think attracted settlers to Nicodemus? How do you think those who stayed were able to turn Nicodemus into a thriving frontier town?*

Source: Daniel Chu and Associates, *Going Home to Nicodemus*. Morristown, NJ: Silver Burdett Press, 1994.

# The Buffalo Go

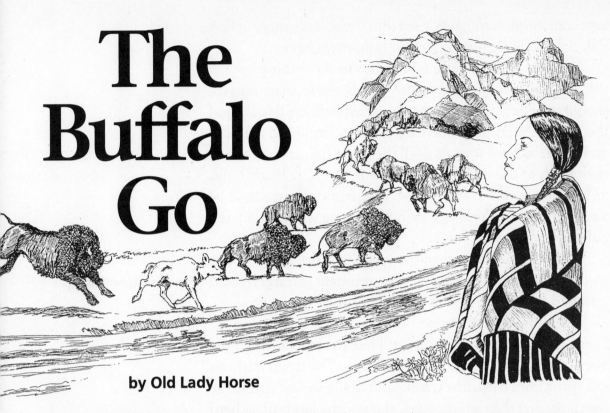

**by Old Lady Horse**

*For hundreds of years giant herds of buffalo roamed the Great Plains of the Middle West. Many Indian groups, such as the Kiowa, depended on the buffalo for food, clothing, and shelter. In the late 1800s hunters began killing all of the buffalo. In the legend below, a Kiowa woman named Old Lady Horse describes what happened to the buffalo and her people.*

Everything the Kiowas had came from the buffalo. Their tepees were made of buffalo hides, so were their clothes and moccasins. They ate buffalo meat. Their containers were made of hide, or of bladders or stomachs. The buffalo were the life of the Kiowas.

Most of all, the buffalo was part of the Kiowa religion. A white buffalo calf must be sacrificed in the Sun Dance. The priests used part of the buffalo to make their prayers when they healed people or when they sang to the powers above.

So, when the white men wanted to build railroads, or when they wanted to farm or raise cattle, the buffalo still protected the Kiowas. They tore up the railroad tracks and the gardens. They chased the cattle off the ranges. The buffalo loved their people as much as the Kiowas loved them.

There was war between the buffalo and the white men. The white men built forts in the Kiowa country, and the . . . buffalo soldiers shot the buffalo as fast as they could, but the buffalo kept coming on, coming on, even into the post cemetery at Fort Sill. Soldiers were not enough to hold them back.

Then the white men hired hunters to do nothing but kill the buffalo. Up and down the plains those men ranged, shooting sometimes as many as a hundred buffalo a day. Behind them came the skinners with their wagons. They piled the hides and bones into the wagons until they were full, and then took their loads to the new railroad stations that were being built, to be shipped east to the market. Sometimes there would be a pile of bones as high as a man, stretching a mile along the railroad track.

The buffalo saw that their day was over. They could protect their people no longer. Sadly, the last **remnant** of the great herd gathered in council, and decided what they would do.

**remnant:** remaining part

The Kiowas were camped on the north side of Mount Scott, those of them who were still free to camp. One young woman got up very early in the morning. The dawn mist was still rising from Medicine Creek, and as she looked across the water, peering through the haze, she saw the last buffalo herd appear like a spirit dream.

Straight to Mount Scott the leader of the herd walked. Behind him came the cows and their calves, and the few young males who have survived. As the woman watched, the face of the mountain opened.

Inside Mount Scott the world was green and fresh, as it had been when she was a small girl. The rivers ran clear, not red. The wild plums were in blossom, chasing the red buds up the inside slopes. Into this world of beauty the buffalo walked, never to be seen again.

*The next selection is a poem about the loss of the buffalo. As you read it, think about what these two pieces have in common.*

Source: Alice Marriot and Carol K. Rachlin, *American Indian Mythology.* New York: Thomas Y. Crowell Company, 1968.

# Buffalo Dusk

**by Carl Sandburg**

*In 1878, when
Carl Sandburg was born
in Galesburg, Illinois, there
were still buffalo roaming
the prairies of North America.
As Sandburg grew up, the Middle West changed. The Plain Indians, who had
depended on the buffalo for survival, were forced onto reservations. The
prairies were turned into farms. The towns grew into cities. By 1920,
when Sandburg's poem "Buffalo Dusk" was published, almost all of the buffalo
were gone. Dusk is the time of day just after sunset, when all of the sunlight
disappears into darkness. Why do you think Carl Sandburg called this poem
"Buffalo Dusk"?*

The buffaloes are gone.

And those who saw the buffaloes are gone.

Those who saw the buffaloes by thousands and how they

pawed the prairie **sod** into dust with their hoofs, their          **sod:** ground

great heads down pawing on in a great **pageant** of dusk,          **pageant:** parade

Those who saw the buffaloes are gone.

And the buffaloes are gone.

*Both Carl Sandburg and Old Lady Horse realized that the end of the buffalo
had changed life in the Middle West forever. Today only a small number of
buffalo still exists.*

Source: Carl Sandburg, *Smoke and Steel*. New York: Harcourt Brace Jovanovich, 1920.

# THE WABASH CANNONBALL

In the middle 1900s the Wabash Cannonball was one of America's best-known trains. The name "Wabash" comes from the Wabash River in the Middle West. Why do you think they called the train the "Cannonball"?

Music by William Kindt
Words adapted by Merrill Stanton

1. From the waves of the At - lan - tic    to the    wild Pa - ci - fic    shore,
*Refrain* Now___    lis - ten to her rum - ble,    now___    lis - ten to her    roar,

From the    coast of Cal - i - for - nia    to    snow - bound La - bra - dor,
As she    ech - oes down the val - ley . and    flies    a - long the shore.

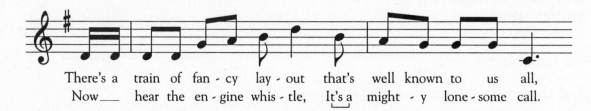

There's a    train of fan - cy    lay - out    that's    well known to    us    all,
Now___    hear the en - gine whis - tle,    It's a    might - y    lone - some call.

It's the    ho - bo's home when he wants to roam___ It's the Wa - bash Can - non - ball.
As we    ride the bars    and the emp - ty cars___ on the Wa - bash Can - non - ball.

2. There's lots of places, partner, that you can go to see.
   St. Paul and Kansas City, Des Moines and Kankakee,
   From the lakes of Minnehaha where the laughing waters fall,
   You can reach them by no other than the Wabash Cannonball. *Refrain.*

3. For years I've ridden on this line across the countryside.
   I've always been well treated, tho' I took the hobo's ride.
   And when my days are over, and the curtains 'round me fall,
   Please ship me off to Heaven on the Wabash Cannonball. *Refrain*

# DOTY'S WASHER

**Advertising Poster from the 1800s**

*In the late 1800s, technology was advancing in leaps and bounds in the United States. Between 1860 and 1900, the first automobiles, telephones, telegraphs, electric lamps, and radios were produced. Cameras and sewing machines, invented in the early 1800s, became popular. People were urged to buy all kinds of wonderful new machines. The advertising poster below shows a washing machine of the 1800s—"Doty's Clothes Washer" with the new "Universal Clothes Wringer." In what ways do you think a new machine like the "Doty's Clothes Washer" changed the lives of women?*

THE PAST.                    THE PRESENT.

## HOUSEKEEPERS, TAKE YOUR CHOICE.

DOTY'S CLOTHES WASHER, lately much improved, and the new UNIVERSAL CLOTHES WRINGER, with Rowell's Expansion Gear, and the patent "Stop," save their cost twice a year by saving clothes, besides shortening the time and lessening the labor of washing nearly one-half.

**A FAIR OFFER.**—Send the retail price:—WASHER, $14; EXTRA COG-WHEEL WRINGER, $9—and we will forward to places where no one is selling, either or both, free of charges. If, after a trial of one month, you are not entirely satisfied, we will REFUND THE MONEY on the return of the machines, FREIGHT FREE.          **R. C. BROWNING, General Agent,**
*Large Discount to the Trade everywhere.*  **32 Cortlandt St., New York.**

# Hitting the Road
# Automobile Advertisements,
## 1902 and 1924

*The first automobiles were invented in the late 1800s. These early cars took a long time to build and cost anywhere from $1,000 to $3,000. Most Americans at that time earned less than $1,000 a year. As a result, only wealthy people could afford to buy cars. Many people, however, benefited from the jobs generated by the new automobile industry. You have read how thousands moved to Detroit and other Great Lake cities to find work with the car manufacturers.*

*When Henry Ford set up an assembly line in his factory in 1913, production time and costs were greatly reduced. Look at the advertisements below. The one on the left is from 1902, and the one on the right is from 1924. How do the cars compare in price and looks?*

The
# Haynes-Apperson

is the only automobile that has been consistently developed through 10 years of successful experience on American Roads.

THE same development that has given foreign cars their reputation has given the Haynes-Apperson its proved reliability, but because of the more severe conditions in this country there is no car of equal horse power that will last as long, handle as easily, and ride as smoothly on American Highways as this American product.

Runabout,  7 Horse Power, 2 Passengers, $1200
Phaeton,  12 Horse Power, 2 Passengers, $1500
Surrey,  12 Horse Power, 4 Passengers, $1800

Ask our Customers        *Delivery in ten days on*
   Get our Booklet        *immediate orders*

## Haynes-Apperson Co., Kokomo, Ind.

*Ford*
**Touring Car**
**$295**

F. O. B. DETROIT
Starter and Demountable Rims $85 Extra

OF all the times of the year when you need a Ford car, that time is NOW!

Wherever you live—in town or country—owning a Ford car helps you to get the most out of life.

Every day without a Ford means lost hours of healthy motoring pleasure.

The Ford gives you unlimited chance to get away into new surroundings every day—a picnic supper or a cool spin in the evening to enjoy the countryside or a visit with friends.

These advantages make for greater enjoyment of life—bring you rest and relaxation at a cost so low that it will surprise you.

By stimulating good health and efficiency, owning a Ford increases your earning power.

Buy your Ford now or start weekly payments on it.

*Henry Ford's automobiles changed life in the United States forever. At such low prices, many people could afford to buy cars. Soon new highways—dotted with gasoline stations, motels, and restaurants—crisscrossed the nation. People used cars to get to work, to go shopping, and to visit friends. With automobiles now available for transportation, many Americans began leaving cities and moving to nearby areas. Suburbs soon began to grow. How do automobiles affect life today?*

# Working the Land

**by Pierce Walker**

*In 1972 the writer Studs Terkel interviewed Pierce Walker, an Indiana farmer. When he was a boy, Pierce Walker lived on a farm of 80 acres. As an adult, he had a farm of 250 acres, and he worked an additional 250 acres for other people. How did Pierce Walker feel about the technology—that is, the new machines— that he used to farm his land?*

Farming, it's such a gamble. The weather and the prices, and everything that goes with it. You don't have too many good days. It scares you when you see how many working days you actually have. You have so many days to get the crop planted and the same in the fall to harvest it. They have this all figured down to the weather. It tenses you up. Whether we needed rain or we didn't need rain, it affects you in different ways. I have seen a time when you're glad to hear the thunder and lightning. Then again, I've wished I didn't hear it. (Laughs)...

Weather will make ya or break ya. The crops have to have enough moisture. If they don't have enough, they hurt. If you have too much, it hurts. You take it like you git. There's nothing you can do about it. You just don't think too much about it. My wife says it doesn't bother me too much. Of course, you still worry....

I don't believe farmers have as much **ulcers** as business people 'cause their life isn't quite as fast. But I'll say there will be more as times goes on. 'Cause farming is changing more. It's more a business now. It's getting to be a big business. It's not the labor any more, it's the management end of it.

**ulcers:** stomach problems

Your day doesn't end. A farmer can't do like, say, a doctor— go out of town for the weekend. He has to stay with it. That's just one of the things you have to learn to live with. I'd say a majority of the time a farmer, when he comes in at night and goes to bed, he's tired enough he's not gonna have trouble sleepin'. Of course, he'll get wore down. . . .

My father-in-law helps me an awful lot in the spring and a little in the fall. He drives the tractor for me. My daughter, she drives a tractor when school is out. When I was home there on the farm, there were five children, three boys, and we were on an eighty-acre farm. It took all of us, my father and three boys. You can see the difference machinery plays in it.

The number of farmers is getting less every day and just seems like it's getting worse every year. The younger ones aren't taking over. The majority of the people **originated** from the farm years ago. But it's been so long ago that the young ones now don't realize anything about the farm. What goes with it or anything like that. The **gamble** that the farmer takes.

**originated:** started

**gamble:** risk

The city people, when they go to the grocery store and the price of meat is raised, they jump up and down. They don't realize what all is behind that. They're thinking of their own self. They don't want to put up that extra money—which I don't blame them either. The same way when I go to buy a piece of equipment. I go jump up and down. . . .

When you get a good crop, that's more or less your reward. If you weren't proud of your work, you wouldn't have a place on the farm. 'Cause you don't work by the hour. And you put in a lot of hours, I tell you. You wouldn't stay out here 'til dark and after if you were punchin' a clock. If you didn't like your work and have pride in it, you wouldn't do that.

You're driving a tractor all day long, you don't talk to anyone. You think over a lot of things in your mind, good and bad. You're thinking of a new piece of equipment or renting more land or buying or how you're going to get through the day. I can spend all day in the field by myself and I've never been lonesome. Sometimes I think it's nice to get out by yourself. . . .

*This interview comes from a book by Studs Terkel. Terkel wanted to know how all different kinds of Americans felt about their jobs, so he traveled around America asking them and tape-recording their answers. If you could interview a farmer in the Middle West today, what questions would you ask?*

Source: Studs Terkel, *Working*. New York: Random House, Inc., 1972.

UNIT

5

# THE SOUTHWEST

*I am a pueblo child and I love*
*to listen to my grandparents*
*tell stories.*

from *Pueblo Storyteller*
by Diane Hoyt-Goldsmith

# Kate Heads West

**by Pat Brisson**

*In Pat Brisson's story, Kate Heads West, Kate is invited to join her best friend Lucy on her family's vacation. Lucy's family is going to tour the Southwest by car. Kate and Lucy learn a lot about the Southwest and have a great time. You can learn about their trip by reading some of the postcards Kate sends back to her friends and family in New Jersey. Which places would you want to visit if you were a tourist in the Southwest?*

*August 6, Fort Worth, Texas*
*Dear Buster and Bruno,*

I hope Brian's keeping your bowl nice and clean like he promised he would. If he threatens to flush you down the toilet, tell him I won't give him the **genuine** cowboy hat I bought for him at the rodeo last night in Fort Worth.

**genuine: real**

My favorite part of the rodeo was the cowgirls racing their horses around barrels in big figure eights. They went around the corners so fast it looked like the horses would fall right over. Lucy and I would probably be world champion barrel-racers if we lived in Texas and owned horses.

Yesterday afternoon we went to a Japanese garden. It was very quiet and peaceful there. Lucy's mom told us the Meditation Garden is just like one she's been to at a temple in Kyoto, Japan. She said it's nice to find a little bit of Japan in Texas. And there were beautiful **imperial carp** swimming in the pools there which reminded me of you.

**imperial carp: a kind of fish that lives in ponds, like a goldfish**

*Your favorite owner,*
*Kate*

P.S. Tell Mom and Dad not to worry—I'm being really polite.

*August 13, On the Road*
*Dear Mom and Dad,*

We're on the longest drive of the vacation — 480 miles from San Antonio to Carlsbad, New Mexico.

Lucy and I sang "The Stars at Night Are Big and Bright, Deep in the Heart of Texas" for the first 100 miles. But then Mrs. T. asked us to do something quiet like count cactus plants. We only got up to sixty-seven.

Then Lucy's dad said we should stop and stretch our legs. Opening the car door was like opening an oven door. My face started baking as soon as I got out. But the air smelled beautiful, not quite like flowers but just as nice.

I thought the desert would be completely empty except for sand. But there are lots of plants, and I saw some birds (but no roadrunners), and two rabbits with the longest ears I've ever seen, and four lizards and some bugs. I was hoping we'd see a **scorpion** or a **tarantula**, but we weren't that lucky.

*Your favorite daughter,*
*Kate*

P.S. Hey, Brian, remember Davy Crockett and the battle at the Alamo? We went there yesterday. It looked a lot bigger on TV.

**scorpion:** a small poisonous animal
**tarantula:** a spider with a painful sting

*August 17, El Paso, Texas*
*Buenos Días, Aunt Mag (that's Spanish for "good day"),*

I'm on vacation in Texas with my friend Lucy and guess what — we *walked* to Mexico yesterday! (We walked from El Paso across the Rio Grande to Juarez.) It was my first time in another country and it was great! I spent the money you gave me on a beautiful skirt, which comes down to my feet, and a blouse with little flowers embroidered all over it. *Muchas gracias!* (That means "thank you very much.")

*Your favorite niece,*
*Kate*

P.S. Here's some more Spanish that I learned: *Dispensame* means "excuse me" and *yo quiero a Mexico!* means "I love Mexico!"

August 18, Buckhorn, New Mexico
Dear Mrs. Heath,

How are things at the library? We visited the Gila Cliff Dwellings National Monument today. We had to climb a narrow trail to get there, and one spot was perfect for hearing your echo from the opposite wall of the canyon. Lucy and I yelled our names to see how many echoes we could get back. (Lucy got six, but I got seven.)

Anyway, the cliff dwellings are stone buildings built right into the side of the cliff. They are about a thousand years old! The Mogollon Indians built them for protection from other tribes. I guess it worked, because they lived here for hundreds of years.

Your favorite reader,
Kate

August 23, the Petrified Forest, Arizona
Dear Brian,

We are having the *best* time! Today we went to the **Petrified** Forest. It wasn't like I expected, but it was still great. I thought there would be all these trees standing around looking like concrete. But there aren't that many trees at all and actually, they're lying around like logs. They look like marbles all melted together—swirls of red and yellow and purple and pink.

I took some great pictures of the petroglyphs (old rock carvings made by the Anasazi Indians). My favorite is a mountain lion with his claws bared and his mouth open in a terrible snarl.

Tomorrow we're going to see the Hopi Snake Dance. Mr. T. said the Hopi dance with live rattlesnakes in their mouths without getting bit. We are also going to visit a pueblo built on a mesa. Mesas are hills with steep sides and flat tops, almost like tables.

Aren't you glad you're my little brother? There's so much you can learn from me.

Your favorite sister,
Kate

**petrified:** changed into stone

August 28, Grand Canyon, Arizona
Dear Mom and Dad,

Thank you, thank you, thank you for letting me come on this trip with Lucy! I can't believe I'll be home in less than a week. We're spending these last days at the Grand Canyon before we fly back. I think they should have named it the Stupendously Gigantic Canyon because it is so unbelievably big. In some places the river is a *mile* down from where we stand—I've even seen birds flying below me. At one lookout point we looked down and saw clouds. Lucy said it was fog, but I think it's the same thing.

We learned so much here that the park ranger gave us Official Junior Ranger Badges!

Yesterday we went river rafting in another canyon. Lucy and I screamed almost the entire trip, and Mr. T. said he had to give our guide a really big tip because we probably broke his eardrums.

Your favorite daughter,
Kate

When Kate returned home at the end of the trip, she had many more stories to tell about the land, the history, and the people of the Southwest. What are some things Kate and Lucy learned about on their trip? Have you ever taken a trip to a different region of the country?

Source: Pat Brisson, *Kate Heads West*. New York: Bradbury Press, 1990.

# The ERRAND

## by Harry Behn

*In Harry Behn's poem, "The Errand," a boy in the Southwest returns a book for his father to a neighboring farmer. His journey turns out to be very special for him. What does the boy see on his journey that is typical of the geography of the Southwest region?*

I rode my pony one summer day  
Out to a farm far away  
Where not one of the boys I knew  
Had ever wandered before to play,  
Up to a tank on top of a hill  
That drips into a trough a spill  
That when my pony drinks it dry  
Its trickling takes all day to fill;  
On to a windmill a little below  
That brings up rusty water slow,  
Squeaking and pumping only when  
A lazy breeze decides to blow;  
Then past a graveyard overgrown  
with gourds and grass, where every stone  
Leans crookedly against the sun,  
Where I had never gone alone.  
Down a valley I could see  
Far away, one house and one tree  
And a flat green pasture out to the sky  
Just as I knew the farm would be!  
I was taking a book my father sent  
Back to the friendly farmer who lent  
It to him, but who wasn't there;  
I left it inside, and away I went!  
Nothing happened. The sun set,  
The moon came slowly up, and yet  
When I was home at last, I knew  
I'd been on an errand I'd never forget.

*Why do you think the poet will never forget the errand he did that day? What errands have you done that you will never forget?*

Source: Harry Behn, *The Golden Hive*. New York: Harcourt, Brace, 1966.

# THE DESERT IS THEIRS

## by Byrd Baylor

*You have read a short excerpt from The Desert Is Theirs on page 287 of your textbook. The following is a longer excerpt from the same poem. In this section, Byrd Baylor writes about the Papagos—the Desert People—as well as the plants and animals that live in the Southwestern desert. What are some of the things that all of the "desert's children" share?*

The desert gives
what it can
to each of its children.

Women weave grass
into their baskets
and birds weave it
into their nests.

Men dig
in the earth
for soil
to make houses—
little square adobe houses
the color of the hills.
And lizards
dig burrows
in the same
safe earth.

Here animals and people know
what plants to eat
when they are sick.
They know what roots
and weeds
can make them well again.

No one has to tell
Coyote or Deer
and no one has to tell
the Papagos.
They share in other ways too.
They share
the feeling
of being
brothers
in the desert,
of being
desert creatures
together.

A year that is hard
for people
is hard for
scorpions too.
It's hard for everything.

Rain is a blessing
counted
drop
by
drop.
Each plant
finds its own way
to hold
that sudden water.
They don't waste it
on floppy green leaves.
They have thorns
and stickers
and points
instead.

**Yucca**
sends roots
searching
far far underground—
farther than you'd ever
   dream
a root
would go.

And **Saguaro** is fat
after rain—
fat with the water
it's saving
inside its great stem.
Give it one summer storm.
It can last a year
if it has to.
Sometimes it has to.

The desert's children
learn to be patient.

Hidden in his burrow,
Kangaroo Rat
spends each long day
waiting
for the heat to fade,
waiting
for darkness
to cool the desert
where he runs.
Just so he runs
   sometime . . .

A weed
may wait
three years
to bloom.
Just so it blooms
   sometime . . .

A toad
may wait
for months
to leave
his sandy hiding place
and sing toad songs
after a rain.
Just so he sings
   sometime . . .

Desert people
are patient too.
You don't see them
   rushing.
You don't hear them
   shouting.

**yucca:** woody-stemmed plant with spearlike leaves and bell-shaped flowers

**saguaro:** giant cactus tree

118

They say you plant
    happier corn
if you take your time
and that squash tastes best
if you've sung it
slow songs
while it's growing.
They do.

Anyway,
the desert has
its own kind of time
(that doesn't need clocks).
That's
the kind of time
snakes go by
and rains go by
and rocks go by
and Desert People
go by too.

That's why
every desert thing
knows
when the time comes
to celebrate.

Suddenly. . .
All together.
It happens.

Cactus blooms
yellow and pink and
    purple.
The Papagos begin
their ceremonies
to pull down
rain.
Every plant joins in.
Even the dry earth
makes a sound of joy
when the rain touches.
Hawks call across the
    canyons.
Children laugh for
    nothing.
Coyotes dance in the
    moonlight.

Where else
would
Desert People
want to be?

*Baylor says that having to wait for rain has taught all desert creatures patience. How does this patience show in the lives of the people, plants, and animals who make their homes in the desert? Can you think of another example of how the way people behave is shaped by the climate of their region?*

Source: Byrd Baylor, *The Desert Is Theirs*. New York: Charles Scribner's Sons, 1975.

# A Geyser of Oil!

## by James A. Clark and Michel T. Halbouty

*This excerpt from a nonfiction book about the hill called Spindletop in Beaumont, Texas, gives an exciting account of what happened on the day that drillers there struck oil. When Patillo Higgins said that an oil deposit would be found beneath the hill, few people believed him. Some even felt sorry for Higgins when he drilled and did not find anything. But one engineer, Captain Anthony Lucas, thought Higgins was right. He leased the land and had a professional drilling crew—made up of Peck Byrd and brothers Al and Curt Hamill—drill a well on the site. The date of the crew's discovery was January 10, 1901. After it, the town would not be the same. A geyser is a natural hot spring from which steam and hot water shoot into the air after being heated underground. Later the word gusher would be used to describe what was seen in Beaumont that day. How do you think the members of the work crew felt before, during, and after the explosion?*

On the hill the crew of three had put on the new **fishtail bit**. That done, the **drill stem** was lowered back into the hole. With the pipe down about 700 feet and Curt Hamill steering it from the double boards forty feet above the **derrick** floor, something began to happen.

Mud started to bubble up over the **rotary table**. Al and Peck backed away when suddenly the force increased and mud spurted high up the derrick. Curt, drenched with mud and **gumbo** grabbed for the ladder and slid down it to safety. All three scampered in different directions. This was a new experience for these old hands of the **Corsicana** field. As they ran, six tons of four-inch pipe came shooting up through the derrick, knocking off the **crown block**. Then the pipe leapt, like activated spaghetti, on over the top of the derrick and broke off in sections, falling around the camp like giant spikes driven into the earth.

**fishtail bit:** cluster of rock-cutting blades at the bottom of a drill

**drill stem:** longest part of the drill

**derrick:** framework over the oil well that supports the drill

**rotary table:** machinery in the derrick floor that turns the drill stem

**gumbo:** sticky soil

**Corsicana:** oil drilling town about 290 miles from Beaumont

**crown block:** pulley system at the top of the derrick

Then everything was quiet. The Hamills and Peck Byrd cautiously returned to the derrick floor. It was a **shambles**, with mud, muck and water standing a foot deep. The disgusted crew looked over the situation [and] started cleaning up the **debris**. . . .

[Suddenly, they] were interrupted by a roar like the shot of a heavy cannon. Then again the flow of mud started up through the hole, followed by a terrific column of gas. The startled crew scattered again. Peck missed his footing and tumbled headlong into the **slush pit**. Within seconds, the gas was followed by a solid flow of oil—green and heavy.

"Peck, run to the house and get the Captain," Al shouted, "while Curt and me try to figure this thing out. It looks like oil! Hurry! Hurry!"

The mud-soaked Peck Byrd ran to the Lucas home. When he got there he was out of breath and sat holding his side, panting a few minutes, before he could deliver the message to **Mrs. Lucas**.

"Get the Captain! Tell him to come right now!" Peck shouted in excitement. "Look, Mrs. Lucas, look," he said, pointing to the well. But before she could find out what had happened, Peck was off on a run back to the well.

She looked toward the hill and saw a great **plume** of black liquid spouting over the derrick. The sight was fantastic. She could not explain what had happened, but she **implored** the Captain to lose no time in getting back to the hill.

"Hurry, Anthony, something awful has happened. The well is spouting," she shouted into the telephone.

The Captain turned and fled from the store without explanation. He mounted his **gig**, as Louie Mayer watched in astonishment, and stood on the floor-boards whipping his horse as he raced out Park Street, past the **O'Brien and Carroll** homes, out Highland Avenue and past his own home without looking toward his wife, who was trying to attract his attention by waving from the porch.

The **phenomenon** was in full view now. It was frightening to the Captain. His eyes had never beheld such a sight before. Could it be oil?

When he reached the hill, Lucas' excitement was too much and the horse was too slow. At the **apex** of the hill, he

**shambles:** place of great disorder

**debris:** remains of something destroyed

**slush pit:** hole that holds mud needed for drilling blades

**Mrs. Lucas:** had encouraged her husband to continue drilling even when he was thinking of giving up

**plume:** shape like a large, fluffy feather

**implored:** begged

**gig:** horse-drawn carriage

**O'Brien and Carroll:** founding partners of the Gladys City Oil Company along with Patillo Higgins

**phenomenon:** extraordinary event

**apex:** highest point

121

tried to jump from the buggy and tumbled down the slope. Al Hamill saw the fall and started toward him, but the Captain rolled forward and came to his feet on a **dead run**.

"Al, Al," he was shouting, "what is it? What is it?"

"Oil, Captain! Oil, every drop of it," the **jubilant** Al replied.

Grabbing Al Hamill by the waist and swinging him around, Lucas looked up toward the gray skies and said, "Thank God. Thank God, you've done it! You've done it!"

"It came in at ten-thirty, almost an hour ago, and it has been shooting a steady six-inch stream of oil more than a hundred feet above the top of the derrick, just like it is now. I can't understand it," Al said. . . .

Captain Lucas was **exultant**. He stood under the shower of green oil, felt it, smelled it and tasted it to make certain he wasn't dreaming.

Then he backed off and looked up to the top of the great plume. Oil, **shale**, and rocks were raining down. Almost to himself he whispered hoarsely, with a rising **inflection**, "A geyser of oil! A geyser of oil!"

**dead run:** very fast sprint

**jubilant:** joyful

**exultant:** rejoicing triumphantly

**shale:** fine-grained rock formed from clay

**inflection:** change in voice pitch

*A local farmer named Charley Ingals saw the gusher, jumped on his horse, and went riding through town, calling "Oil on the hill! Oil on the hill!" Townspeople came running out to see. Ingals was not happy about the oil ruining his farmland, though. He sold his land for $1,500—a move he would later regret. Many other local farmers, ranchers, and businesspeople became rich after the discovery of "black gold" in Beaumont. And some 40,000 people moved to the town to work in the booming oil industry. Why is oil, or petroleum, so valuable? What are some of its uses?*

Source: James A. Clark and Michel T. Halbouty, *Spindletop*. New York: Random House, Inc., 1952.

# PUEBLO STORYTELLER

**by Diane Hoyt-Goldsmith**

*April Trujillo, a Pueblo girl living in a small town near Santa Fe, New Mexico, was ten years old when she told her story to Diane Hoyt-Goldsmith. In this excerpt from the book* Pueblo Storyteller, *April describes some of the Pueblo traditions she has learned. What do her grandparents' stories teach April?*

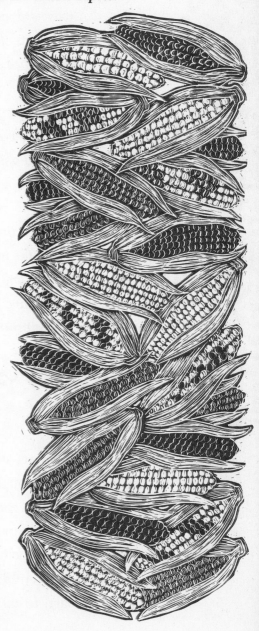

For me there is a special time at the end of the day. After the work is finished and I am ready to go to bed, my grandmother and grandfather tell me stories from the past. Sometimes they tell about the legends of the pueblo people. Other times they tell about things that happened in their own lives.

My grandmother likes to tell about when she was a girl. She lived in a Tewa (tay' *wah*) pueblo to the north called San Juan. She remembers autumn, a time when her whole family worked together to harvest and husk the corn crop. The corn came in many colors—red and orange, yellow and white, blue and purple, and even the deepest black.

Her family would sit in the shade of a ramada (rah-mah'-dah) built of cedar branches. Sheltered from the hot sun, the workers would remove the husks from a mountain of colorful corn. All the time they were working, they would laugh at jokes, sing songs, and share stories.

My grandmother tells me there were always lots of children around—her brothers and sisters, their cousins and friends—and they always had fun. My grandfather tells how the boys would use their slingshots to hurl stones at the crows who came too close to the corncobs that were drying in the sun.

When I was very young, my grandparents told me a legend about how our ancestors found the place where we are living today, our pueblo along the Rio Grande River. They call it "How the People Came to Earth," and it is still one of my favorite tales.

# HOW THE PEOPLE CAME TO EARTH

*Long, long ago, our people wandered from place to place across the universe. Their leader was Long Sash, the star that we call Orion. He was the great warrior of the skies. Long Sash told his people that he had heard of a land far away, a place where they could make a home.*

*Because the people were weary of wandering, they decided to follow Long Sash on the dangerous journey across the sky to search for a new home. They traveled on the Endless Trail, the river of countless stars that we call the Milky Way.*

*The way was hard for our people. Long Sash taught them to hunt for food, and to make clothing from the skins of animals and the feathers of birds. Even so, they were often hungry and cold, and many died along the way. Long Sash led them farther than any people had ever gone before.*

*After a time, the people came to a vast darkness, and they were afraid. But Long Sash, the great warrior, believed they were heading the right way, and led them on. Suddenly, they heard the faint sound of scratching. Then, as they watched, a tiny speck of light appeared in the distance. As they got nearer, the light grew larger and larger. Then they saw that it was a small hole leading to another world.*

*When they looked through the opening, they saw a little mole digging away in the earth. Long Sash thanked the mole for helping them to find their way out of the darkness. But the mole only replied, "Come in to our world. And when you see the sign of my footprints again, you will know you have found your true home." The people saw a cord hanging down from the hole and they all climbed up and went through into the new world.*

My grandparents are storytellers who have brought the past alive for me through their memories, through their language, through their art, and even through the food we eat. I am thankful that they have given me this rich history. From them I have learned to bake bread in an ancient way, to work with the earth's gift of clay, and to dance to the music of the Cochiti drums.

I am a pueblo child and I love to listen to my grandparents tell stories. From their example, I learn to take what I need from the earth to live, but also how to leave

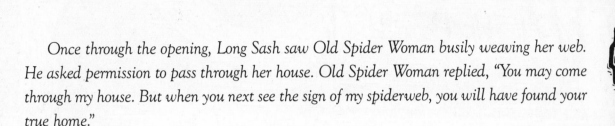

Once through the opening, Long Sash saw Old Spider Woman busily weaving her web. He asked permission to pass through her house. Old Spider Woman replied, "You may come through my house. But when you next see the sign of my spiderweb, you will have found your true home."

The people did not understand what Old Spider Woman meant, but they thanked her and continued on their journey.

Long Sash and his followers traveled to many places on the earth. They found lands of ice and snow, lands where the sun burned and the air was dry, and beautiful lands with tall trees and plenty of game for hunting. In all of these places, they searched for signs of the mole and Old Spider Woman, but found nothing.

Some of the people stayed behind in the lands they discovered, but Long Sash and most of the tribe kept going. They kept searching for their true home.

Finally they came to a new land where the seasons were wet and dry, hot and cold, with good soil and bad. They found, here and there, small tracks that looked like a mole's. They followed the tracks and found a strange-looking creature, with ugly, wrinkled skin. The slow-moving animal carried a rounded shell on its back.

Long Sash was very happy when he saw the creature. "Look!" he said. "He carries his home with him, as we have done these many years. He travels slowly, just like us. On his shell are the markings of the spiderweb and his tracks look just like the mole's."

When our people saw the turtle, they knew they had found the homeland they had traveled the universe to discover. And we still live on those same lands today.

something behind for future generations. Every day I am learning to live in harmony with the world. And every day, I am collecting memories of my life to share one day with my own children and grandchildren.

*Perhaps there is someone who reads to you or tells you stories. Do you like hearing stories? Why is storytelling different from watching television or going to a movie?*

Source: Diane Hoyt-Goldsmith: *Pueblo Storyteller*. New York: Holiday House, 1991.

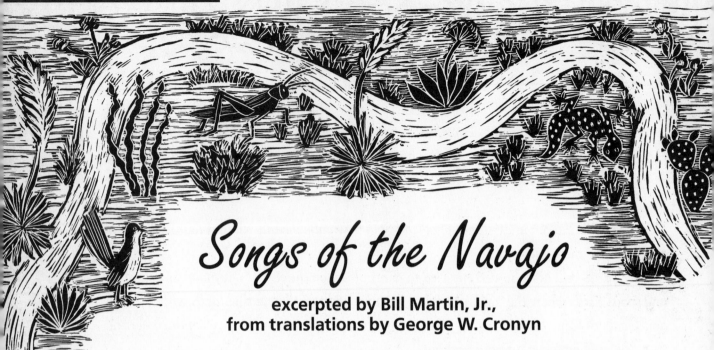

# Songs of the Navajo

### excerpted by Bill Martin, Jr.,
### from translations by George W. Cronyn

*The Navajo's respect for the beauty of nature is expressed in this traditional chant. What do you think the speaker's definition of beauty would be? What is yours?*

In beauty may I walk.
All day long may I walk.
Through the returning seasons may I walk.
On the trail marked with pollen may I walk.
With grasshoppers about my feet may I walk.
With dew about my feet may I walk.
With beauty may I walk.
With beauty before me, may I walk.
With beauty behind me, may I walk.
With beauty above me, may I walk.
With beauty below me, may I walk.
With beauty all around me, may I walk.
In young age wandering on a trail of beauty,
   lively, may I walk.
In old age wandering on a trail of beauty,
   lively, may I walk.
It is begun in beauty.
It is begun in beauty.

*The chant also expresses the connections between one season and the next and between youth and old age. What do you think is meant by the last line, "It is begun in beauty"?*

Source: Bill Martin, Jr., *Sounds of the Storyteller.* New York: Holt, 1972.

# Spanish Pioneers of the Southwest

**by Joan Anderson**

*The Spanish were the first Europeans to settle in the Southwest. The following is an excerpt from a book about a Spanish settlement called El Rancho de las Golandrinas (EL RAHN choh de las goh lahn DREE nahs), near what is now Santa Fe, New Mexico. Miguel Baca is a young child in the family that lives on the ranch in the middle 1700s. The Baca family farms, raises sheep, and runs an inn for travelers. Although they are on good terms with their Pueblo neighbors, they are fighting with the nearby Navajo. Miguel's older brother, Pedro, has been taken captive in a Navajo raid. Miguel wonders about what Pedro is doing, even as he tries to take his place on the ranch. What is a day like for Miguel?*

It was warm and cozy in the Bacas' *cocina*. The chili stew smelled **delectable** as the family gathered and **Abuelita** Luisa dished it up. Everyone sat quietly, exhausted but content to be slowing down from the toils of the day.

The chill of the night descended upon them. Emilio Baca built up the fire as his wife, Isabel, unrolled the blankets and sheepskins that would become their beds. Miguel's father took his place atop the fireplace, and the others huddled close to the hearth.

Miguel felt his muscles relax as his mother began to sing softly to the baby. For the first time all day, Miguel knew he was safe. Only here in the cozy *cocina* did he feel he could let his guard down. He couldn't let Papá know that he

*cocina* (koh-SEE nah): kitchen
**delectable**: delicious
**Abuelita** (ah bwe LEE tah): Grandma

127

wasn't all that brave. So on the outside, Miguel stood tall and proud, but on the inside he trembled with fear.

Dawn came early. With only a few tiny windows in the Bacas' *cocina*, it was impossible to know when the sun came up. But the **patrón** took care that the people of Golondrinas were alerted to the early hour by ringing the **hacienda**'s huge iron bell.

*patrón* (pah TROHN): landlord, boss

**hacienda** (ah see EN dah): ranch house

Miguel stirred upon hearing the dull clang. One. Two. Three. Four. Five. On the fifth ring he bolted upright. Glancing about the room he saw that Papá's bed was vacant! Was he already at work? Miguel quickly rolled up his blanket, gulped down a cup of **atole**, and headed out the door.

*atole* (ah TOH LE): cornflour porridge

Sure enough, Papá was down by the stream near the small plot of **cultivated** farmland. Miguel ran as fast as he could, anxious to show his father that even though he wasn't as big and strong as Pedro, he was eager to work.

**cultivated:** prepared, tilled

"I'm here, Papá," he announced. "What shall I do?"

"Quickly, grab hold of the yoke while I secure it to their horns. These beasts want nothing of work this morning."

Miguel did as his father said, and eventually they attached the **crude** wooden plow and headed for the far end of the field. The earth was hard and dry. Miguel was always amazed that things grew in such unhealthy-looking soil.

**crude:** rough, homemade

"Papá," he asked, his teeth chattering in the early morning chill, "isn't it still too cold for planting?"

"It would seem so, my son," Emilio Baca answered as the **plowshare** dug into the soil and began to turn the earth. "But we must hope that the days soon become warm, as it takes many months to grow our corn and beans and wheat. Besides, **Padre** José will come to bless our fields during the **Feast of San Ysidro**. If we haven't done our work there can be no blessing, *sí*?"

**plowshare:** front edge or blade of plow

**Padre** (PAH dre): Father, priest

**Feast of San Ysidro** (SAHN ee SEE droh): holiday celebrating the coming of spring

"I suppose not, Papá," Miguel answered, working steadily now. It felt good to be sharing chores with someone instead of being alone tending sheep and collecting wood. Time passed quickly, and by late afternoon they were putting in the seed. Miguel felt proud of their accomplishment, especially since the *patrón* had been watching their progress from the rooftop on the hacienda....

During the next few days, Miguel went about his regular chores hoping that soon the *patrón* would remember his promise and permit him to stand watch in the **torreón**.

Each morning he tossed fresh straw into the **corral** for the barn animals to eat. He fed the chickens and turkeys, milked the goats, and held the sheep steady while they were sheared.

In the afternoons, sometimes with his father, sometimes alone, he took the sheep to the nearby hills to graze. The days were long and hard, and Miguel began to wonder why there seemed to be more work this spring than in other years. Then he realized—Pedro wasn't there this year to share in all the work. . . .

[One morning] all regular chores were put aside so that the villagers could prepare for the festival. Padre José was needed in other settlements and would stay for only a day or two.

The saint maker of Golondrinas had been working day and night in anticipation of the padre's arrival. His beautiful carving of San Ysidro plowing the fields was almost complete. Miguel loved to watch as he mixed brightly colored paints from different plants and chipped away at a block of wood until the block disappeared and in its place was a magnificent figure. Tomorrow San Ysidro, the patron saint of farmers, would be carried about the hacienda on his way to the little chapel. From this spot, high above Golondrinas, he would bless and watch over the fields until harvest.

Nearby, Doña María was hunched over a bunch of dried chilis, picking out the seeds and grinding them into powder. Blue corn would be ground as well to make flour for all the tortillas that would be consumed at the fiesta. **Polonia** stood patiently beside the **hornos** waiting for the **dulces** to bake. Everyone loved the sweet-tasting bread that was made for special occasions.

Finally, it was May 15; the Feast of San Ysidro was upon them.

A procession formed and the crowd moved slowly out of the great pine gate. Carrying the statue of San Ysidro on their shoulders, they wove their way down the hillside to

**torreón** (toh re OHN): large tower, fort

**corral:** fenced-off space for animals

**Polonia:** a Navajo servant in Miguel's village who has adopted Spanish ways. Miguel wonders if his brother Pedro has similarly adopted Navajo ways.

**hornos** (OR nohs): ovens

**dulces** (DOOL ses): sweet, dessert breads

the precious **irrigation ditch**, around the newly planted field of crops, through the pasture, until finally they approached the chapel. They chanted as they walked.

**irrigation ditch:** hole where water is stored

San Ysidro, land tiller
Protect our crops
From pests and storms
San Ysidro, golden whiskered
Pray to God
To send us rain in torrents

Miguel watched as they placed the wooden saint gently on the altar of the tiny church. From there, San Ysidro could watch the hacienda and all of its people.

After the ceremony, the padre stood off to the side, his mind deep in thought.

"Padre," Miguel said, "already since your arrival it seems to me that the soil looks richer."

"My boy," Padre José answered, "this is good land that God has given to us to settle upon. If we care for it, taking only what we need, as our Pueblo Indian neighbors do, it will serve us with **abundance**."

**abundance:** plenty

*Miguel looks forward to the Feast of San Ysidro and works hard to prepare for it. What role did religion play in the life of Spanish settlers in the colonial Southwest?*

Source: Joan Anderson, *Spanish Pioneers of the Southwest.* New York: E.P. Dutton, 1989.

# BILL PICKETT

**Cowboy Movie Poster**

*Cowboys herd cattle, protecting them and leading them to good lands for grazing. Some also perform in rodeos. The most famous rodeo cowboy of all was Bill Pickett. Pickett was half African American and half Chocktaw Indian. He was known for roping cattle, riding broncos, and bulldogging. Pickett could jump on top of a bull, grab its horns, and wrestle it to the ground. What does this movie poster tell you about Bill Pickett?*

## An American Cowboy Song

*Many people think that "dogies" are dogs—but "dogies" is the name cowboys used for the motherless calves that strayed from the herds on the long drives from Texas to the railroads. When the cowboys drove their herds north, they sang to themselves and to each other. Sometimes, as in this song, the cowboys sang to the dogies! How does the music sound like cattle moving along?*

1. As I was out walk - ing one morn - ing for pleas - ure,
2. Well it's ear - ly in spring - time we round up the do - gies,
3. The night is a - comin' and the do - gies are stray - in',

132

I saw a young cow - boy a - rid - ing a - long;
We train them to fol - low and nev - er to stray;
They're far - ther from home ____ than they've been be - fore;

His hat was thrown back and his spurs were a - jing - lin',
Then load the chuck wag - ons with beans and with ba - con,
Come on lit - tle do - gies, it's time to be roll - in',

And as he ap - proached he was sing - ing this song.
And as soon as there's day - light we'll be on our way.
When we get to Wy - o - ming we'll roll ____ no more.

*Refrain*

Whoop-ee ti - yi - yo, git a - long, lit - tle do - gies,

It's your mis - for - tune and none of my own;

Whoop-ee ti - yo - yo, git a - long, lit - tle do - gies,

For you know Wy - o - ming will be your new home.

# THE TEXAS SPIRIT

**by Barbara Jordan**

*Barbara Jordan was one of the Southwest's celebrated "rugged individuals."
She stood by what she believed and was not afraid to take chances. Jordan was
elected to the United States House of Representatives in 1972. Her victory was
unusual because at the time very few African Americans or women were
representatives. In fact, Jordan was the first African American to be elected by
Texas to the House of Representatives. After leaving that position in 1979,
Jordan continued to work hard to create more opportunities for all people. In
1989 Brian Lanker interviewed Barbara Jordan for his book I Dream a World.
How does Jordan's life reflect the "spirit of Texas"?*

**W**hen I was a student at Texas Southern University
in Houston, I had to ride the bus from my house to school
across town. There was a little **plaque** on the bus near the back
that said **"Colored"** and when I'd get on I'd have to go all the
way back to that little plaque and I was passing empty seats all
the time.

**plaque:** sign

**colored:** old word for
African Americans

In 1962, I lost a contest for the state House of Representatives. And some of the people were saying that I probably lost
the race because people are just not **accustomed to** voting for
a woman. And I just said, "Well, now, that is totally ridiculous
and I'll just have to try to **alter** that."

**accustomed to:** used to

**alter:** change

134

All my growth and development led me to believe that if you really do the right thing, and if you play by the rules, and if you got enough good, solid judgment and common sense, that you're going to be able to do whatever you want to do with your life. My father taught me that.

The civil rights movement called [upon] America to put a giant mirror before it and look at itself. I believe that the movement said to America, "Look at what you have been saying to us black people all of these years. Look what you have been trying to sell us as the bill of goods for America. Look at that and then ask yourselves, have you really done it? Do the black people who were born on this soil, who are American citizens, do they really feel this is the land of opportunity, the land of the free, the home of the brave, all that great stuff?"

And when America looked into that giant mirror and heard these questions, the drumbeat—that's what the movement was, this drumbeat of questions—America had to say, "No, I really haven't, as a country, lived up to what I've said this country could be for you." And so the civil rights movement was a time of requiring that America be honest in its promises. And that was the goodness of the movement.

I am telling the young people that if you're dissatisfied— and I don't think they can be students in a school of public affairs and not be dissatisfied—if you are dissatisfied with the way things are, then you have got to **resolve** to change them. **resolve:** decide I am telling them to get out of there and occupy these positions in government and make the decisions, do the job and make it work for you. . . .

Texas is more than a place. It is a frame of mind. A Texan believes that the individual is powerful. Texas has that rugged individualism. It may not be polished, may not be smooth, and it may not be silky, but it is there. I believe that I get from the soil and the spirit of Texas the feeling that I, as an individual, can accomplish whatever I want to and that there are no limits, that you can just keep going, just keep soaring. I like that spirit.

*In 1979 Barbara Jordan became a professor at the University of Texas in Austin. Her students there have said that Jordan always carried a copy of the United States Constitution with her. Barbara Jordan died in 1996 at the age of 59. What do you think she will be remembered for?*

Source: Brian Lanker, *I Dream a World*. New York: Stewart, Tabori & Chang, 1989.

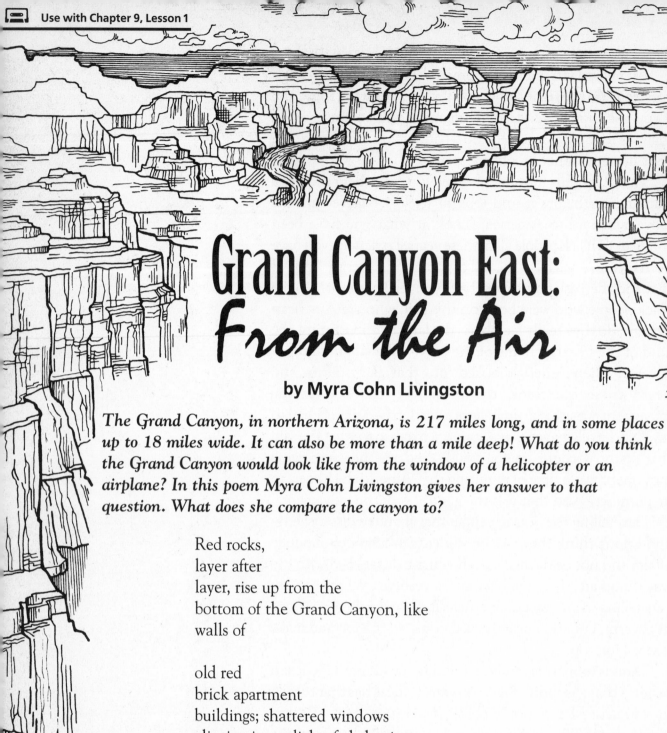

# Grand Canyon East: From the Air

## by Myra Cohn Livingston

*The Grand Canyon, in northern Arizona, is 217 miles long, and in some places up to 18 miles wide. It can also be more than a mile deep! What do you think the Grand Canyon would look like from the window of a helicopter or an airplane? In this poem Myra Cohn Livingston gives her answer to that question. What does she compare the canyon to?*

> Red rocks,
> layer after
> layer, rise up from the
> bottom of the Grand Canyon, like
> walls of
>
> old red
> brick apartment
> buildings; shattered windows
> glinting in sunlight; faded paint
> peeling.

*Do you get the sense that the poet is starting at the bottom of the canyon and rising up? Why or why not? What about the Grand Canyon do you think she compares to "shattered windows"? What makes her think of "faded paint peeling"? How might the images be different if she had described the Grand Canyon "from the ground"?*

Source: Myra Cohn Livingston, *Remembering and other poems.* New York: Macmillan Publishing Co., 1989.

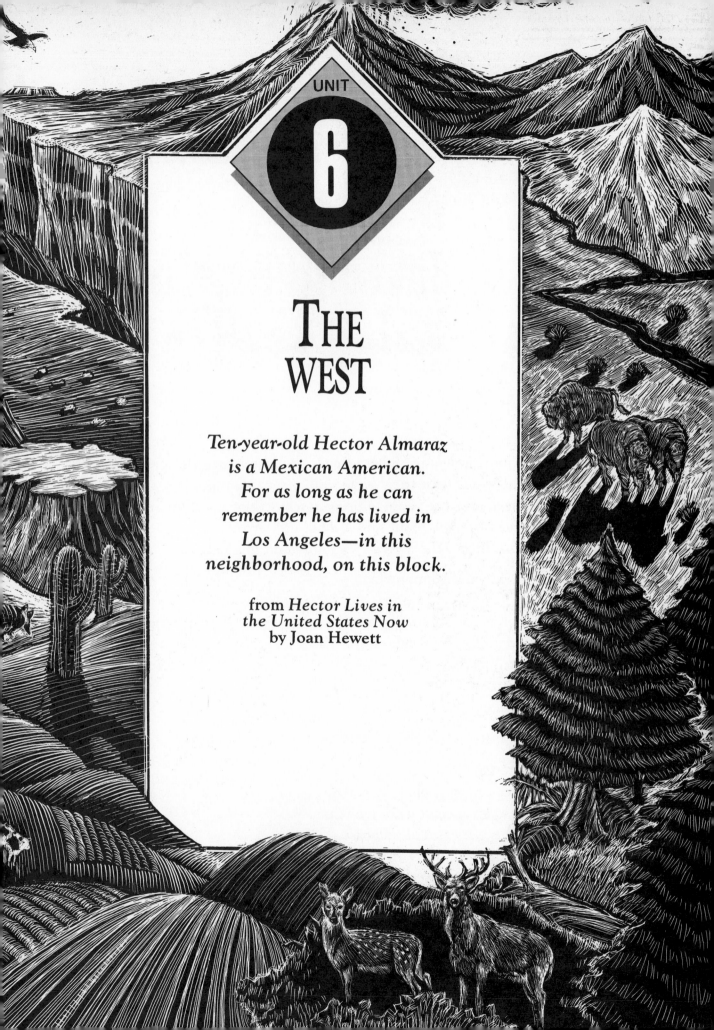

# THE WEST

Ten-year-old Hector Almaraz
is a Mexican American.
For as long as he can
remember he has lived in
Los Angeles—in this
neighborhood, on this block.

from *Hector Lives in
the United States Now*
by Joan Hewett

# SIERRA

**by Diane Siebert**

*In her poem "Sierra," Diane Siebert traces the history of the Sierra Nevada mountains. She begins with their birth millions of years ago and then describes how they changed over the years to become what they are today: a beautiful site with a great variety of plant and animal life. What are some of the plants and animals that live in the Sierra Nevada mountains today?*

I am the mountain,
　　　Tall and grand.
And like a **sentinel** I stand.　　　　**sentinel:** guard
Surrounding me, my sisters rise
With watchful peaks that **pierce** the skies;　　**pierce:** cut
From north to south we form a chain
Dividing desert, field, and plain.
　　　I am the mountain.
　　　　Come and know
Of how, ten millions years ago,
Great forces, moving plates of earth,
Brought, to an ancient land, rebirth;
Of how this planet's **faulted crust**　　**faulted:** cracked or
Was shifted, lifted, tilted, thrust　　　broken, resulting in
Toward the sky in waves of change　　　earthquakes
To form a newborn mountain range.　　**crust:** Earth's
　　　I am the mountain,　　　　outermost layer
　　　　Young, yet old.

138

I've stood, and watching time unfold,
Have known the age of ice and snow
And felt the **glaciers** come and go.                    **glaciers:** huge sheets
They moved with every melt and freeze;                        of ice
They shattered boulders, leveled trees,
And carved, upon my granite rocks,
The terraced walls of **slabs** and blocks                 **slabs:** big, flat pieces
That trace each path, each downward course,                    of rock
Where through the years, with crushing force,
The glaciers sculpted deep **ravines**                     **ravines:** valleys
And polished rocks to glossy sheens.
At last this era, long and cold,
Began to lose its **frigid** hold                          **frigid:** icy
When, matched against a warming sun,
Its final glacier, ton by ton,
Retreated, melting, making way
For what I have become today:
A place of strength and **lofty** height;                  **lofty:** very high
Of shadows shot with shafts of light;
Where meadows nestle in between
The arms of forests, cool and green;
Where, out of **clefted** granite walls,                   **clefted:** creased
Spill silver, snow-fed waterfalls.
Here stand the pines, so straight and tall,
Whose needles, dry and dying, fall
Upon my sides to slowly form
A natural blanket, soft and warm;
Their graceful, swaying branches sing
In gentle breezes, whispering
To **junipers**, all **gnarled** and low,                  **junipers:** evergreen
That here, in stubborn splendor, grow.                        shrubs or trees
And on my western slope I hold                             **gnarled:** knotted
My great **sequoias**, tall and old;                       **sequoias:** tallest trees
They've watched three thousand years go by,                   in the world
And, in their endless **quest** for sky,                   **quest:** search
This grove of giants slowly grew
With songs of green on silent blue.
        I am the mountain.
          In each breath
I feel the pull of life and death                          **predator:** an animal
As untamed birds and beasts obey                              that hunts other
The laws of **predator** and **prey**.                        animals
                                                           **prey:** animals hunted
                                                              by predators

On me, the hunted ones reside,
Sustained by foods my plants provide:
I keep the **pikas,** small and shy,
That spread their gathered grass to dry.
I shelter rodents. In my trees
Live pinecone-loving **chickarees,**
While tunnels, **crevices,** and holes
Hold **marmots,** ground squirrels,
   chipmunks, **voles.**
I cradle herds of graceful deer
That drink from waters cold and clear;
I know each **buck** with antlers spread
Above his proud, uplifted head.
I know each doe, each spotted fawn,
In sunshine seen, in shadows, gone.
I know these creatures, every one.
They, to survive, must hide or run;
As food for those that stalk and chase,
Within life's chain, they have a place.
Then, too, the predators are mine,
Each woven into earth's design.
I feel them as they wake and rise;
I see the hunger in their eyes.
These are the coyotes, swift and lean;
The bobcats, shadowy, unseen;
The **martens** in their tree-branch trails;
The masked raccoons with long, ringed tails;
The mountain lions and big black bears
That live within my rocky **lairs;**
The owls that prowl the skies at night;
The hawks and eagles, free in flight.
I know them all. I understand.
They keep the balance on the land.
They take the old, the sick, the weak;
And as they move, their actions speak
In tones untouched by right or wrong:
      We hunt to live.
      We, too, belong.
     I am the mountain.
      From the sea
Come constant winds to conquer me—
Pacific winds that touch my face

**pikas:** small rodents similar to rabbits

**chickarees:** red squirrels

**crevices:** narrow openings

**marmots:** mountain mice

**voles:** a kind of rodent

**buck:** male deer

**martens:** animals like weasels

**lairs:** dens

And bring the storms whose clouds embrace
My rugged shoulders, strong and wide;
And in their path, I cannot hide.
And though I have the strength of youth,
I sense each change and know the truth:
By wind and weather, day by day,
I will, in time, be worn away;
For mountains live, and mountains die.
As ages pass, so, too, will I.
But while my cloak of life exists,
I'll **cherish** winds and storms and mists,
For in them, precious gifts are found
As currents carry scent and sound;
As every gust and playful breeze
Helps **sow** the seeds of parent trees;
As silver drops and soft white flakes
Fill laughing streams and alpine lakes;
As lightning fires, hot and bright,
Thin undergrowth, allowing light
To reach the fresh, cleared soil below
So roots can spread and trees can grow.
        I am the mountain,
            Tall and grand,
        And like a sentinel I stand.
Yet I, in nature's wonders **draped**,
Now see this mantle being shaped
By something new—a force so real
That every part of me can feel
Its actions changing nature's plan.
Its numbers grow. Its name is MAN.
And what my course of life will be
Depends on how man cares for me.
        I am the mountain,
            Tall and grand.
        And like a sentinel I stand.

**cherish:** love and treasure

**sow:** spread, scatter

**draped:** dressed

*Diane Siebert says that "MAN" is a new force whose actions change nature's plans. What does she mean by this? She says that the life of the Sierra Nevada mountains depends on how man cares for them. How do you think that people can take care of mountains?*

Source: Diane Siebert, *Sierra*. New York: HarperCollins, 1991.

# ROLL ON, COLUMBIA

**by Woody Guthrie**

*There are many songs that describe the beauty of this country's rivers, but this is one of the few that describes how we use our rivers for electric power. In the late 1930s, many people in this country did not have electricity. The United States government started a program that helped bring hydroelectric power to the western United States. Woody Guthrie, a famous folk singer, wrote this song to celebrate the Columbia River. What does Guthrie mean when he says, "Your power is turning our darkness to dawn"?*

*Words by Woody Guthrie*

*Music based on "Goodnight Irene" by Huddie Ledbetter and John Lomax*

1. Green Doug-las fir where the wa-ters cut through,
2. Oth-er big riv-ers add___ pow-er to you,

Down her wild moun-tains and can-yons she flew.
Yak-i-ma, Snake, and the Klick-i-tat, too.

Source: Woody Guthrie, *Roll On, Columbia*. New York: Ludlow Music, Inc. 1936.

# A Walk Through My Rain Forest
## by Isaac Olaleye

*This poem was written about a rain forest in Nigeria. In what ways could the poem apply to the Amazon rain forest in Brazil? How is the forest described in the poem similar to the forests of the West in our country? How is it different?*

A walk through my rain forest is haunting.
Its greatness makes me feel very small.
What I see
Of its brilliant beauty
Is more than can be described.

I walk into a hidden, green paradise—
Paradise within paradise.
Every corner reveals
Unexpected wonders!

Its ponds are crowded
By a blizzard of butterflies.
Everywhere there is music—
The sounds of rivers,
A rustling of leaves,
An outpouring of mockingbirds,
And the forlorn cooing of turtledoves.

The rain forest is the home
Of **exotic** plants: resurrection lily,
Snakewood and zigzag begonia.

**exotic:** strangely beautiful, unusual

The rain forest is my home,
A palace of fragrance and tastes
That delight the senses.
Where the rain forest begins
And ends
Is pure paradise.
When I turn to leave,
The trees wave
Good-bye!

*What are some of the "unexpected wonders" the poet sees in the rain forest? What do you think he means when he says that "the trees wave good-bye!"?*

Source: Isaac Olaleye, *The Distant Talking Drum*. Honesdale, PA: Boyds Mill Press, 1995.

# When the Wind Blows Hard

by Denise Gosliner Orenstein

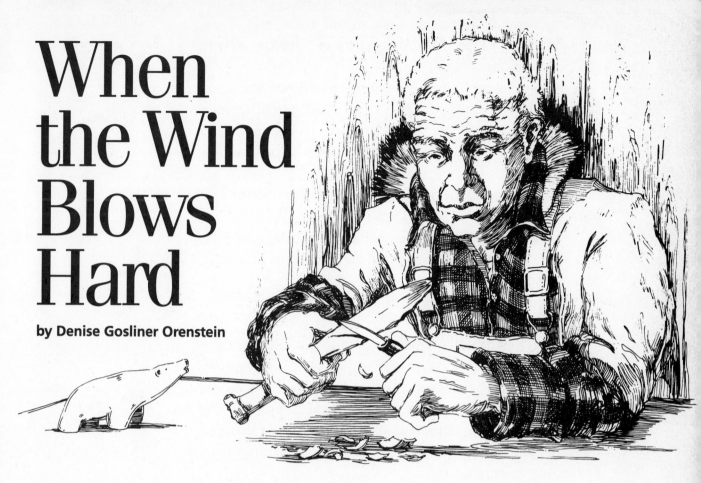

*The way of life of Native Americans in Alaska has changed over the last hundred years, but many of their traditions survive. In the novel* When the Wind Blows Hard, *a girl named Shawn moves with her family from New York City to Alaska. Shawn is unhappy in the small town of Klawock. Her Tlingit classmates think that her red hair is strange, and Shawn thinks her classmates seem different too. Soon, however, a Tlingit girl named Vesta becomes Shawn's best friend. In the selection below, Shawn makes another friend—Vesta's grandfather. The older man is skilled at a traditional Tlingit craft, the carving of totem poles. Each animal shown on the totem pole has a special meaning. Why do you think the grandfather tells Shawn about the mosquito?*

When I got to his house, I knocked on the door, waited for a minute, and then walked in. Vesta's grandfather was sitting at the table, just like before. He was cutting a piece of wood with a knife. Just like before. There was no reason to be nervous.

"Hello, young Shawn," he said.

"Hello," I said, setting his dinner down on the table. "I brought you something to eat. I thought you might like some more dinner tonight. This time, I made your dinner all by myself. My mother is at a teachers' meeting tonight."

Vesta's grandfather might have smiled just a little. It was hard to tell. He put one hand on my arm and pointed to a chair.

"Sit down," he said.

I sat down next to him. He picked up the piece of wood again and began cutting it with a knife. I had seen other men in Klawock cut wood like that. It's called carving. It's a kind of artwork. Vesta's grandfather began to talk as he carved. This is what he said:

"This wood is like the pulse of a wrist. It's full of motion and warm inside the hand. What I am carving is alive."

I watched the piece of wood change shape as he carved. It looked like magic. All at once, I could see the shape of a small, curved paddle.

"Are you carving a paddle?" I asked.

He nodded.

"This is a paddle like those from long ago. All we had to move our boats in those days were paddles. We had no engines. Even then, we carved our paddles like pieces of art. When I was small, like you, my uncle taught me to carve as I am carving now. My uncle was an artist and taught me not to do anything halfway. The Tlingit people treat art as something alive, something to be respected."

Vesta's grandfather had a way of speaking that really made you listen. Maybe it was because he spoke so softly. Maybe it was because he didn't speak often. Kind of like Vesta.

"Have you ever carved a totem pole?" I asked.

Vesta's grandfather nodded. "The totem pole in Klawock with the red fox on top, I carved that."

I couldn't believe it. The fox totem pole was my favorite. He continued talking.

"A person who makes totem poles has learned to study the animals. First, I had to study the fox. The fox is a lively creature and runs around like a small child. The fox is a symbol of a child."

He smiled and touched my hair.

"Your hair is red, like the color of the fox. You are lively and fast like the small animal the Tlingit people admire."

It was so nice to hear him say that. It made me feel warm.

"Did you paint the totem poles you carved?" I asked. "Totem poles are so big, so tall, how did you reach way up to paint them?"

Vesta's grandfather laughed.

"You paint the totems when they are lying down across the earth," he said, "before they are placed upright to stand in the sky. Long ago, we used paint brushes made from wild bushes and made all different kinds of paints from the nature around us. Some paints were made from tree bark, some from blueberries and blackberries. These old Indian paints last for hundreds of years. They never fade in the sun. Now, these paints from long ago are gone. Very few people remember them. But the totems remain."

"What do the other totem pole animals mean?" I asked. "Besides the fox totem?"

He was quiet for a moment.

"The crab is the symbol of the thief because he has so many hands. The mosquito represents teaching. When a mosquito bites, you start itching. Sometimes learning hurts."

He put the paddle down on the table next to the dinner I had brought and looked at me.

"This paddle is for you," he said. "Take it home. It will let you hear the sounds of long ago."

I felt funny. The paddle was so beautiful, but I didn't feel right taking the carving home. He picked up the paddle and handed it to me. It felt warm, warm from the heat of his hands.

"The Tlingit does not turn down any gift," he said, "but accepts it with open arms."

That is when Vesta's grandfather and I finally became friends.

Walking home that evening I buttoned my jacket right up to my chin. It was getting colder; maybe the snow would be here soon. The cool air felt good on my cheeks and through the tangles of my red hair. A very thin frost—not quite ice, not quite snow—had covered the hill behind the school yard where the totem poles stood. I walked up the hill slowly, carefully, until I reached the top. The totem poles surrounded me in a large circle and I could hear the faraway hum of water brushing the shore. A quick wind blew hard and my ears stung a little from the cold, but I didn't put up my hood. I looked straight up at the totem poles and felt the small paddle in my jacket pocket. Something was shining in my heart.

*A few months later, Shawn gets some sad news. Vesta and her parents are moving away from Klawock. Shawn thinks she'll never be happy there again. But after Vesta leaves, Shawn continues her friendship with Vesta's grandfather. She tells him, "You and I will . . . be each other's special family." After a while, she finds she doesn't miss New York City that much, and she loves Alaska, "even when the wind blows hard."*

Source: Denise Gosliner Orenstein, *When the Wind Blows Hard*. Reading, Massachusetts: Addison-Wesley, 1982.

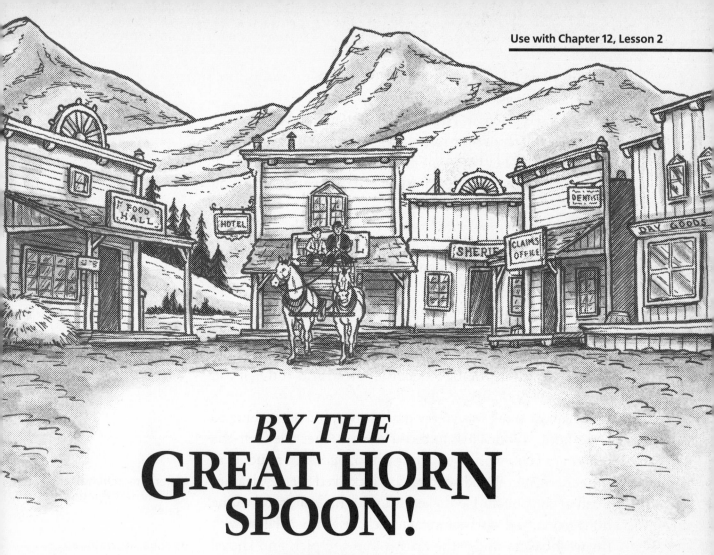

# BY THE GREAT HORN SPOON!

**by Sid Fleischman**

*Excitement ran high in the gold fields of California in 1849. People could have no money one day and be worth $1 million the next day if gold was discovered on their claim! But it didn't always work out that way. Sid Fleischman's novel* By the Great Horn Spoon! *takes place during the California Gold Rush. It is a work of historical fiction. The characters are made up, but the historical details are accurate. In this section 12-year-old Jack Flagg and Praiseworthy, the family butler, have just arrived in California. Their goal is to return to Boston with enough money to save the family home. What do they discover about life in the mining camps?*

There was road dust in Jack's eyebrows, in his ears and down his neck. Now that they had arrived he had gold fever so bad that he didn't see how he could wait another five minutes to get his shovel in the ground. . . .

It was exactly one hour and five minutes before Jack saw the **diggings**. First Praiseworthy registered at the hotel. They washed . . . "Can we go now?" said Jack, fidgeting. He had polished his **horn spoon** so much he could see his nose in it.

**diggings:** where the Forty-Niners panned for gold

**horn spoon:** a spoon made from a deer's antlers

149

"Go where?"

"The diggings."

"Oh, the diggings will still be there after lunch, Master Jack."

Praiseworthy's patience was a marvel—and an **exasperation**. They had come more than 15,000 miles and now they had to stop to eat. Jack didn't care if they passed up eating for a week. A month, even . . . .

"You and the boy want bread with your **grub**?" asked the waiter. He was a big fellow in floppy boots.

"Why not?" answered Praiseworthy.

"It's a dollar a slice."

The butler slowly arched an eyebrow.

"Two dollars with butter on it."

Praiseworthy peered at Jack, and then smiled. "Hang the cost, sir. We're celebrating our arrival. Bread and butter, if you please!"

The bear steak was greasy and stringy, but something to write home about. Jack forced it down. After they left the restaurant Praiseworthy bought a pair of buckskin pouches at the **general merchandise** store. . . . Jack liked the new leather smell of the pouch. He tucked it under his belt, next to the horn spoon, and was beginning to feel like a miner. Then, with tin **washbasins** under their arms and the pick and shovel across their shoulders, they set out for the diggings.

The day was hot and sweaty. When they reached running water they saw miners crouched everywhere along the banks. They were washing gold out of the dirt in everything from wooden bowls to frying pans.

"Anybody digging here?" asked Praiseworthy when they came to a bare spot.

"Shore is," came the answer. "That's Buffalo John's claim."

The butler and the boy moved on upstream . . . .

On and on they went, looking for a place to dig. They passed miners in blue shirts and red shirts and checked shirts and some in no shirts at all. Picks assaulted the earth and shovels flew. Weathered tents were staked to the hillsides and the smell of boiling coffee drifted through the air. After they had walked a mile and a half Jack began to think they would never find a patch of ground that wasn't spoken for.

Suddenly a pistol shot cracked the mountain air. Praiseworthy's washbasin rang like a bell and leaped from his arm and went clattering away.

"You there!" a voice from behind bellowed.

Praiseworthy turned. His eyes narrowed slowly. "Are you talking to me, sir?"

"Talkin' and shootin'. What you doin' with my washpan under your arm?"

Jack stared at the man. He had a thick, tangled beard and his ears were bent over under the weight of his slouch hat.

"Needless to say, you're mistaken," Praiseworthy answered. "Until this moment I've had the good fortune never to set eyes on you or your washpan, sir."

"We don't take kindly to thievery in these parts," growled the miner, stepping forward. "A man steals around here, we lop off his ears. That's miner's law."

"Do you have any laws against shooting at strangers?"

"Nope."

Jack couldn't imagine Praiseworthy with his ears lopped off. He took a grip on the handle of the shovel as the miner came closer. His heart beat a little faster and he waited for a signal from Praiseworthy.

The miner belted his pistol and picked up the washpan. He **crimped** an eye and looked it over.

**crimped:** squinted

"It's mine, all right."

"You're either near-sighted or a scoundrel," said Praiseworthy.

Jack was ready to fight, if not for their lives—at least for Praiseworthy's ears. Just then, a flash of tin in the sunlight, from a pile of wet rocks, caught Jack's eye. He dropped the shovel and went for it.

"Is this your pan?" Jack said.

The miner's bushy eyebrows shot up like birds taking wing. "It is at that, ain't it?" Then he laughed as if the joke were on him. "I'd forget my boots if I didn't have 'em on."

Praiseworthy peered at the man. Apparently, shooting at strangers by mistake didn't amount to anything in the diggings. The miner hardly gave it another thought.

*Forty-Niners didn't usually include children and family servants. But in some ways Praiseworthy and Jack were typical Forty-Niners. They came to California to get rich quick and leave. And just like the other Forty-Niners, Jack and Praiseworthy realized it was not going to be nearly as easy as they had hoped.*

Source: Sid Fleischman, *By the Great Horn Spoon!* Boston: Little, Brown and Company, 1963.

# THE HEAVY PANTS OF MR. STRAUSS

### by June Swanson

*One of the unexpected results of the Gold Rush was blue jeans, which were created in California in the 1850s for gold miners. Levi Strauss made and sold hundreds and hundreds of these pants to the Forty-Niners, who needed strong clothing so that they could pan for gold. "The Heavy Pants of Mr. Strauss" is an essay by June Swanson that describes how blue jeans were invented during the Gold Rush. The advertisement shown on page 153 is from 1880 but is still used today. Early advertisements bragged that blue jeans were so strong that even two horses pulling in opposite directions couldn't pull the pants apart! Do you think this is why people buy blue jeans today?*

On January 24, 1848, gold was discovered at Sutter's Mill in California. Almost overnight people were coming to California by the thousands, hoping to make a fortune in the new gold fields. In one year San Francisco grew from a small town to a city of 25,000 people. By 1850 the territory had a population of almost 100,000, and in that year California became the thirty-first state.

The new miners needed many things, and usually they had the money to buy whatever they wanted. This **abundance** of people with money to spend brought a great number of **peddlers** and merchants to California. One of these peddlers was a man named Levi Strauss.

**abundance:** great number

**peddlers:** traveling salesmen

In 1850 Levi Strauss made the long trip from the east coast to California by boat. The trip took him all the way around the southern tip of South America. With him, Levi Strauss brought yards and yards of heavy canvas to make tents for the miners and covers for their wagons.

However, when Strauss arrived in California, he found that the miners needed good, heavy pants much more than they needed tents. None of the pants available were tough enough to stand up against the rocks of the California hills and the hard

152

mining life. So Levi, seeing the possibility for a good business, made his tent canvas into pants instead of tents.

Strauss's tent canvas was a bit stiff for pants, so he began to make his pants out of a tough but less stiff material that he had sent to him from Nimes (Nēm), France. The material was called *serge de Nimes*. Serge is a kind of material, *de* means "from," and Nimes is the name of a city in France. Soon *serge* was dropped from the name, and the material was called *de Nimes*, or "denim."

The miners liked the denim pants so much that Levi couldn't make them fast enough. In fact, his pants were so well made that their basic design hasn't changed in over 100 years. Somewhere along the way they came to be called by their maker's first name—"Levi's."

Today the company that Levi Strauss began during the 1860s is still making the same basic straight-legged, button-fly, denim pants that he originally designed for the miners of California. Levi's have become so popular that they are sold (and copied) all over the world.

*Blue jeans became very popular all over the United States. Today they are made by many different companies and sold all around the world. Since Levi Strauss invented blue jeans in 1850, over 2 billion pairs of jeans have been sold.*

Source: June Swanson, *The Spice of America*. Minneapolis: Carolrhoda Books, Inc., 1983.

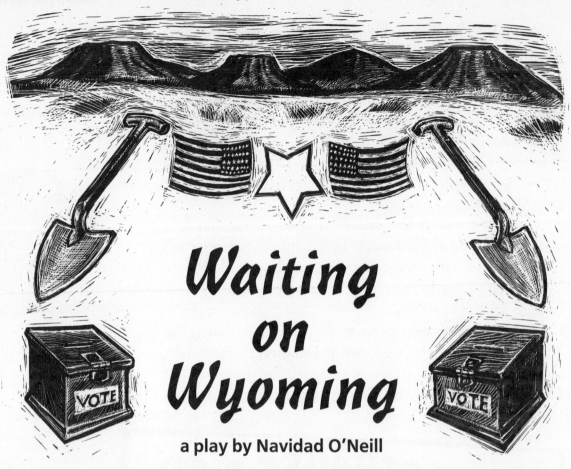

# Waiting on Wyoming

## a play by Navidad O'Neill

*You have read that until 1919 women could not vote in national elections. The struggle for voting rights—or suffrage— for women gained support in the West, where men and women worked side by side and many people were open to new ideas. The territory of Wyoming passed a law in 1869 allowing women to vote in its elections, making it the first place in the country where women could vote. This play takes place on the day the first ballots were cast by Wyoming women. Why was this such an exciting moment? How did people in other parts of the country feel about this event?*

CAST OF CHARACTERS
**Esther Morris**
**Mr. Morris,** her husband
Son 1
Son 2 } *the Morrises' sons*
Son 3
**Reporter**
**Grandma Swain**
**Poll Attendant**
**Miner**
**Chorus** of newspaper editors
**Editor 1**

**Time:** *Early morning, December, 10, 1869.*
**Setting:** *The Morrises' general store in the territory of Wyoming.*

*One area should be identified as a polling place, and another as a kitchen. The chorus, seen throughout the play, should be located in a newspaper office, "back East."*

*At the store, Son 1 and Esther tug at a CLOSED sign. The other members of the Morris family look on.*

**Son 1:** But Ma, today is December Tenth!

**Mr. Morris:** I agree, Esther. No one will mind if you close the shop.

**Son 2:** You've been working so hard for this day to happen. You've been talking to all the legislators, talking to the neighbors . . .

**Esther:** But people depend on this store. I am going to open it for them, like I do every day, even though today *is* the first day the women of Wyoming will vote in an election.

**Mr. Morris:** The first day women *anywhere* in our country will vote.

**Esther:** That's true but you know what I say: Neither rain, nor snow, nor fleet of rattlesnakes can close my shop.

*She turns the sign from CLOSED to OPEN. Reporter comes rushing in.*

**Reporter:** The mail in?

**Mr. Morris:** Came early this morning.

*Mr. Morris pulls out a large sack of letters.*

**Esther:** I've already taken my letters.

*She shows a large pile. Mr. Morris empties his sack, begins sorting the letters.*

**Reporter:** Wow! There's enough of them, isn't there? Why, here's a letter from my editor.

**Son 3:** Mama, what's an editor?

**Esther:** An editor runs a newspaper. Decides what stories should be
written.

**Mr. Morris:** And whether the stories are important enough to go on the
front page.

**Reporter:** Listen to this:

*Editor 1 steps out of chorus. As Reporter reads we hear Editor speak.*
*Lines could also be divided up among chorus members.*

**Editor 1:** Dear Dan, my man, in Wyoming.
We want to hear all about what happens when women vote
for the first time. Everyone back East expects that there will be
many problems. Wyoming is so new and seems pretty rough to us
back home in the East. Is it true there aren't even cobblestones on
the street yet? Is it true that there are miners who actually sleep on
the side of mountains to protect their claims? How will such men
act when they have to share their voting rights? Let us know
everything. We also want to know who will be the first woman
to vote.

*Grandma Swain enters the shop as the Reporter continues to read.*

**Editor 1:** Get her name. What she says. Especially any trouble that
happens. It's up to you, Dan, my man. We will hold our breath
until we hear from you. We plan on sharing your stories with other
newspapers up and down the coast. Send us a telegraph as soon as
you can.
**Reporter:** You bet I will.

**Chorus:** We're waiting. We're waiting.
Waiting on Wyoming news!
We're waiting. Anticipating.
Send us hints, please! Send us clues!

**Grandma Swain:** Lovely morning isn't it?

**Esther:** Good morning to you, Grandma Swain.

**Grandma Swain:** Yes, it is a good morning and I plan to enjoy every minute of it. Esther, I'll take one of those tins of blueberry preserves on that top shelf of yours.

**Esther:** Sure, Grandma Swain. Anything else?

**Grandma Swain:** Any cherry syrup?

**Esther:** One last bottle.

**Grandma Swain:** I'll take that too.

*She pays for the purchases.*

**Esther:** Why the special ingredients, Grandma Swain? This isn't your usual grocery order.

**Grandma Swain:** I'm fixing myself a red, white and blue breakfast today.

*Grandma Swain exits. Walks over to her kitchen area.*

**Son 2:** Good thing we had the store open, Ma. Grandma Swain would have been disappointed if we had been closed.

**Son 3:** What are all those other letters?

**Reporter:** All seem to be predictions.

**Son 1:** What's a prediction?

**Reporter:** When a person announces beforehand what is going to happen later.

**Son 3:** But no one knows the future.

**Mr. Morris:** A lot of people think they do, like that editor who thinks that just because the mountains are rugged, people living in Wyoming must all be rough too.

**Chorus:** We're waiting. We're waiting.
  Waiting on Wyoming news!
  We're waiting. We're waiting.
  For that place to blow a fuse!

*Grandma Swain in her kitchen.*

**Grandma Swain:** Two cups of flour...one cup of blueberries. Mix well.

**Reporter:** You see, son, there are suffragists and anti-suffragists.

**Son 2:** I know Mama's a suffragist because she wants women to vote.

**Son 1:** So does an anti-suffragist not want Mama to vote?

**Mr. Morris:** An anti-suffragist doesn't want *any* women to vote.
  Including herself, if she is a her.

**Reporter:** And anti-suffragists want me to include their predictions in
  my story.

*Reporter rips open a letter.*

**Reporter:** They say: If women have the right to vote, they will leave
  their kitchens and hang out on the street smoking cigars all day.

**Son 2:** You'd never do that, would you, Ma?

**Esther:** You know I hate cigar smoke.

*Grandma Swain is now eating pancakes.*

**Grandma Swain:** Hmmmm. Hmm. Blueberry pancakes with cherry
  syrup and whipped cream. For a star-spangled morning.

*Reporter rips open another letter.*

**Reporter:** They say: Women don't know enough about current events
  to vote wisely.

**Son 3:** But Ma keeps up with what's happening, just like Pa.

*Reporter rips open another letter.*

**Reporter:** Here's another. They say: If women try to vote on December 10th, there will be fights. Some angry men will try to stop the women at the poll booths.

**Sons 1, 2, 3:** Ma, maybe you shouldn't vote!

**Esther:** Well, children, I say, the country is like a general store. If there's an OPEN sign on the door, then anyone can come in and do business. You don't hang a CLOSED sign up for some customers and an OPEN sign for others. But it's taking a while for our country to open the election place to all. It used to be closed to men who didn't own property. And until recently it was closed to African American men. And it's still closed to all women.

*Grandma Swain has finished eating. She stands up.*

**Grandma Swain:** I've waited 75 years for this day.

**Chorus:** We're waiting. We're waiting.
Waiting on Wyoming news!
We're waiting. Anticipating.
What should we, back East, conclude?

*Enter a miner with a shovel.*

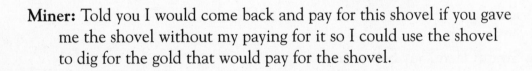

**Miner:** Told you I would come back and pay for this shovel if you gave me the shovel without my paying for it so I could use the shovel to dig for the gold that would pay for the shovel.

**Esther:** I knew you would. You're an honest man.

**Miner:** Okay if I pay in gold nuggets?

**Esther:** Sure.

*Miner pays in gold nuggets.*

**Miner:** And I thank you for trusting me. Trust is what makes a person feel part of the community. Now I'm off to find some more gold.

**Esther:** Well, good luck to you. And your shovel.

**Miner:** And I want you to know, Esther Morris, I never voted in any election before. But today I'm planning on voting, too. I figure if you think it's so important—then, well, maybe it is.

*Miner exits.*

**Mr. Morris:** Boys, 'you think you can handle things at the store while your mother and I go to cast our votes?

**Sons:** Sure.

**Son 2:** We love to be in charge!

**Reporter:** Do you mind if I go with you?

**Esther:** The more the merrier.

*They all move from the store onto the street area.*

**Mr. Morris:** Look, there's Grandma Swain.

*Grandma Swain at the polling place. She folds a piece of paper and hands it to poll attendant.*

**Grandma Swain:** Here's my ballot, sir.

**Poll Attendant:** Why thank you kindly, Grandma Swain. You can put it right in the box.

**Grandma Swain:** *(She does.)* I hope I've served as an example. Voting is the peaceful way to make changes. *(She walks up to the group. To Reporter:)* Write that in your story.

**Reporter:** I will.

*They all shake hands.*
*They freeze in this celebratory position, except Reporter who speaks to the*
*audience as he writes with his pencil on a pad.*

**Reporter:** The first woman to vote in the country was an elderly
   Quaker woman, known to all as Grandma Swain.

*Grandma Swain unfreezes and continues the story.*

**Grandma Swain:** She began an election process that was very peaceful
   throughout the territory of Wyoming—as quiet as the folding of a
   paper ballot.

**Poll Attendant:** Twenty-one years later, when Wyoming was to become
   a state, the United States Congress asked that Wyoming repeal
   the right to vote for women, since the rest of the country did not
   allow it.

**Mr. Morris:** Wyoming refused. It said it would rather wait another
   100 years to become a state than become a state denying women
   the right to vote.

**Chorus:** No more waiting! Anticipating!
   The answer has come in:
   Women in Wyoming win!

**Esther:** I guess you could say that on that day in Wyoming the polling
   places were finally "open." (*She holds up the sign.*) But now our play
   is "closed." (*She turns sign over to CLOSED.*)

## THE END

*Esther Morris of Wyoming was later elected as the first woman judge in the*
*United States. These important events gave Wyoming the nickname "Equality*
*State." What do you think it was about life in the West that made people eager*
*to accept equality for women?*

# Hector Lives in the United States Now

**by Joan Hewett**

*The border between Mexico and the United States is 1,900 miles (3,057 km) long. Many people cross this border every day. People from Mexico often come to the United States in order to get work because there are more jobs available in the United States than in Mexico. In her book Hector Lives in the United States Now, Joan Hewett writes about a real boy named Hector Almaraz, whose parents came to the United States to find work when Hector was a small boy. Hector and his parents were born in Mexico, but they have lived in Los Angeles, California, since Hector was about two years old. What special role does Hector play in his family?*

*T*en-year-old Hector Almaraz is a Mexican American. For as long as he can remember he has lived in Los Angeles—in this neighborhood, on this block.

Hector's parents are Leopoldo and Rosario Almaraz. He also has three brothers: nine-year-old Polo, and Miguel and Ernesto, who are seven and four.

Hector and Polo were born in Guadalajara, Mexico, and are Mexican citizens, like their parents. Their younger brothers,

162

Miguel and Ernesto, were born in Los Angeles and are American citizens.

When Hector's parents came to California to find work, they did not understand English. But they had heard so much about Los Angeles, from sisters and brothers and their own parents, that the city seemed almost **familiar**.

At first they stayed with relatives. Then Leopoldo found a job, and the family moved to Eagle Rock, a **residential section** of the city.

They are still there. The streets and parks are safe, and an elementary school and a Catholic church are only a few blocks from their small, **bungalow-style** apartment.

Hector has lots of friends. Most of them live on this block. They play together after school and on Saturdays and Sundays.

Soccer is one of their favorite games. So is baseball. When it is baseball season, they dig out a bat, ball, and glove and practice batting in a backyard or alley. Other times they go to the park to play volleyball, or just to see what is going on. If no one has a flat, they ride their bikes over; otherwise they walk.

Like his friends, Hector likes to read comic books and collect baseball cards. Sometimes they gather their cards or books, meet on the front stoop, and trade. Although the children talk and joke in English, their parents come from Mexico and Central America, and Spanish is the language spoken in their homes.

When Hector and Polo are drawing or doing their homework at the kitchen table, they often tell stories to each other in English. They speak as fast as they can so their mother will not understand them. Rosario gets annoyed because she suspects they do it just to tease her.

Although Hector and Polo speak English equally well, their parents think it proper that their eldest boy be the family **spokesperson**. Hector enjoys the responsibility. Whenever someone who can only speak English telephones them, Hector is called to the phone. Or when Rosario has to get a **prescription** filled at the drugstore, Hector goes along to talk to the **pharmacist**.

Hector did not speak English when he started kindergarten. It was a scary time. He was away from his mother and brothers. He understood only a few English words and did not know

**familiar:** something you know

**residential section:** neighborhood where people live

**bungalow-style:** houses that are one-story high

**spokesperson:** person chosen to speak for the group

**prescription:** medicine order

**pharmacist:** druggist

163

what was going on in class. In first grade Hector had trouble learning to read. But he was **determined** to learn English, and by the end of the second grade he was reading and writing as well as his classmates. School started to be fun.

determined: to have your mind made up

Now Hector is a fifth grader, one of the big kids. In United States history, his class is reading about the different immigrant groups who helped settle the West. Their teacher says, "We are a nation of immigrants. Indians, also called Native Americans, have lived here for thousands of years. Everyone else has come to the continental United States from some other place." Then she smiles and says, "Let's find out about us."

The students in Hector's class are told to ask their parents about their ancestors and then write a brief history of their families. It is an exciting project. When they finish their reports, they will glue snapshots of themselves to their papers and hang them on the wall. But first they get to read them aloud.

Philip traces his family back as far as his great-great-great-grandmother. His ancestors lived on a small Philippine island. Many of them were fishermen. Philip, his sister, and his parents are the only people in his family who have settled in the United States.

One side of Nicky's family came from Norway and Germany. His other ancestors came from Ireland and Sweden. All of them were farmers, and when they came to this country they homesteaded land, which means they farmed and built a house on **uncultivated** public land that then became theirs under a special homestead law.

uncultivated: unfarmed

Vanessa's great-great-grandmother was a Yaqui Indian from Sonora, Mexico. Her grandfather fought in the Mexican Revolution. Another one of her ancestors was French.

Erick is descended from Ukrainian, German, and Italian immigrants. His German grandfather and Ukrainian grandmother met in a prisoner-of-war camp. When they were released, they married and came to the United States by ship.

Julie is of French, Irish, and Spanish descent. Her Great-Great-Grandma Elm was born in Texas. When Elm was a child her family moved to California. They traveled by covered wagon.

Everyone is interested in Kyria's family history. One of her African ancestors was a soldier in the American Revolution. Another fought for the Confederacy in the Civil War. Other members of her family homesteaded in Oklahoma.

Hector tells the class about his Mexican ancestors. They were farmers and carpenters.

There are twelve other Mexican-American children in Hector's class, and some two hundred fifty thousand Mexican-American students in Los Angeles schools....

Hector always tries to complete his homework during study period. When he can't, he finishes it at home. Hector's parents had only a grade school education, and his grandparents did not go to school at all. Hector knows that he is the first one in his family to have the chance to go on to high school, and he does not **intend** to let his family down.

**intend:** plan

Hector does not know yet what he wants to do after high school, but computers **intrigue** him, and he wonders if he might like working with them.

**intrigue:** interest

A few months ago he took a short beginner's computer lesson so that he could use the computers at his local public library. The library has computer games, and for a while he had great fun playing them. Then they seemed too simple. But he read a book about the different kinds of things computers can do and is looking forward to taking a real computer course when he's a little older.

Before Hector started using the library's computers he had only been to the library once, on a trip with his whole class. Now it is a place he visits regularly. Polo and Victor, one of his neighborhood friends, go with him. They take out books on building kites and drawing dinosaurs. And after watching TV dramas about John F. Kennedy, Robert Kennedy, and Martin

Luther King, Jr., Hector read books about them.

Because Hector is curious about past events and famous public figures, his parents gave him a thick, hardcover book about the last one hundred years of United States history. When no one is leafing through it, the book sits on a special shelf beside an English dictionary. Aside from the dictionary, it is the first English-language book Hector's family has purchased. . . .

One Saturday Leopoldo and Rosario announce that the whole family will be going to Guadalajara. Not this summer, because Leopoldo can't get off from work then. They will be going over Christmas vacation!

Hector is thrilled. He will see his grandparents and his aunts and uncles. He will be with Guadalupe, the cousin he has been writing to. His papa says they will take their van or go by bus. Either way, they will get to really see Mexico. And either way, he will get out of school two weeks early.

Leopoldo and Rosario talk about how happy they will be to see everyone. Starting Friday they will begin saving a little money each week so they can buy Christmas presents for everyone they will visit in Mexico. The boys want to know more about the trip.

Finally they run out of questions. Leopoldo leaves for the video store, taking Polo and Miguel with him. Rosario starts to make chili. Ernesto goes outside to play. And Hector and his friends head for the park.

*In 1988 Hector and his parents applied for United States citizenship. Do you know of any well-known person who was born in another country and now lives in the United States? Which country did that person come from? Why did that person come to the United States?*

Source: Joan Hewett, *Hector Lives in the United States Now.* New York: J. B. Lippincott, 1990.

# *A Mountain View*

## by Rose Burgunder

*The Sierra Nevada mountain range is one of the natural beauties of the American West. Much of the range is in eastern California. The range is 400 miles long and up to 80 miles wide. Due to their high elevation, the Sierras are snowcapped all year. The speaker of this poem enjoys the light and the look of the sunset on the mountain range. Why do you think the speaker wants everything to stay just as it is for a little while longer?*

Sunset.
Sierra Nevada:
snow on the soft blue range.

Sky, keep your glittering
moon for a while—
don't let the mountains change.

*What is the sunset like where you live? How do the landforms or buildings of your region look in the changing light of the sun?*

Source: Rose Styron, *From Summer to Summer*. New York: Viking Press Inc., 1965.

# INDEX BY *Category*

# INDEX BY *Subject*

# ACKNOWLEDGMENTS

*(continued from copyright page)*

"Knoxville, Tennessee" from BLACK FEELING BLACK TALK BLACK JUDGEMENT by Nikki Giovanni. ©1968 by Nikki Giovanni.

"Buffalo Dusk" from SMOKE AND STEEL by Carl Sandburg. ©1920 by Harcourt Brace Jovanovich, Inc., renewed 1948 by Carl Sandburg. Harcourt Brace Jovanovich, Inc.

"City, City" from THAT WAS SUMMER by Marci Ridlon. ©1969 by Marci Ridlon McGill.

Excerpts from KATE HEADS WEST by Pat Brisson. Text ©1990 by Pat Brisson. Bradbury Press, an Affiliate of Macmillan, Inc.

Excerpt from WALK ACROSS AMERICA by Peter Jenkins. Text ©1979 by Peter Jenkins. William Morrow & Company, Inc.

Excerpt from WHEN THE WIND BLOWS HARD by Denise Gosliner Orenstein. ©1982 by Denise Gosliner Orenstein.

WHEN I WAS YOUNG IN THE MOUNTAINS by Cynthia Rylant. ©1982 by Cynthia Rylant. Penguin USA Inc.

Excerpt from ROSA PARKS: MY STORY by Rosa Parks. ©1992 by Rosa Parks. Penguin USA Inc.

"I, Too" from COLLECTED POEMS by Langston Hughes Copyright © 1994 by the estate of Langston Hughes, reprinted by permission of Alfred A. Knopf, Inc.

Excerpt from WORKING by Studs Terkel. ©1972, 1974 by Studs Terkel. Pantheon Books, a division of Random House, Inc.

"The Errand" from THE GOLDEN HIVE by Harry Behn. ©1957, 1962, 1966 by Harry Behn.

Excerpt from I DREAM A WORLD by Brian Lanker. ©1989 by Brian Lanker. Stewart, Tabori & Chang, Publishers.

"Roll on, Columbia" words by Woody Guthrie. ©1936 (renewed 1964), 1950 (renewed 1985) and 1963 Ludlow Music, Inc. New York, NY.

Excerpt from 50 SIMPLE THINGS KIDS CAN DO TO SAVE THE EARTH by John Javna. ©1990 by John Javna. Andrews & McMeel.

"States and Capitals" by Professor Rap. ©1990 by Professor Rap.

"The Wabash Cannonball" words adapted by Merrill Staton, music by William Kindt. ©1986 and 1987. Rockhaven Music.

Excerpt from BY THE GREAT HORN SPOON! by Sid Fleischman. ©1963 by Albert S. Fleischman. Little, Brown and Company.

"I See the Promised Land" speech by Martin Luther King, Jr., from A TESTAMENT OF HOPE *The Essential Writings of Marting Luther King, Jr.,* edited by James Melvin Washington. ©1986 by Coretta Scott King, Executrix of the Estate of Martin Luther King, Jr.

"Pueblo Storyteller" from PUEBLO STORYTELLER by Diane Hoyt-Goldsmith. Text ©1991 by Diane Hoyt-Goldsmith. Holiday House.

"Bringing the Praire Home" by Patricia MacLachlan from THE BIG BOOK FOR OUR PLANET. ©1993 Patricia MacLachlan. Dutton's Childrens Books, a division of Penguin Books USA Inc., NY.

From SEQUOYAH'S GIFT by Janet Klausner. ©1993 Janet Klausner. HarperCollins Children's Books, a division of HarperCollins Publishers, Inc.

"John Greehow's Store: Willliamsburg, Virginia" from WILLIAMSBURG CRADLE OF THE REVOLUTION by Ron and Nancy Goor. ©1994 Ron and Nancy Goor. Atheneum, a division of Macmillan Publishing Company, NY.

"The Brave Conductor" from MANY THOUSANDS GONE: AFRICAN AMERICANS FROM SLAVERY TO FREEDOM by Virginia Hamilton. ©1993 Virginia Hamilton. Alfred A. Knopf, Inc., NY.

"Fall" from DOGS AND DRAGONS/TREES & DREAMS by Karla Kuskin. ©1980 Karla Kuskin. Harper & Row, Publishers, Inc., NY.

"The Long Trail" by Monica Mayper from A NEW ENGLAND SCRAPBOOK: A JOURNEY THROUGH POETRY, PROSE, AND PICTURES by Loretta Krupinskil. ©1994 Monica Mayper. HarperCollins Children's Books, a division of HarperCollins Publishers, Inc., NY.

"Blow, Ye Winds, on the Morning" from SEA TO SHINING SEA. Traditional, arranged by Jerome Epstein. ©1993 Amy L. Cohn. Scholastic Inc., NY.

"Turtle's Race With Bear" from TURKEY BROTHER AND OTHER IROQUOIS FOLK STORIES. Retold by Joseph Bruchac. ©1975 The Crossing Press, Trumansburg, NY.

"Paul Revere's Ride" by Henry Wadsworth Longfellow from ANTHOLOGY OF AMERICAN POETRY. ©1983 Crown Publishers, Inc., Avenel Books.

From I WAS DREAMING TO COME TO AMERICA: MEMORIES FROM THE ELLIS ISLAND ORAL HISTORY PROJECT. Selected by Veronica Lawlor. ©1995 Veronica Lawlor. Viking, a division of the Penguin Group, NY.

From SKYLARK by Patricia MacLachlan. ©1994 Patricia MacLachlan. HarperCollins Children's Books, a division of HarperCollins Publishers, NY.

From GOING HOME TO NICODEMUS by Daniel Chu and Bill Shaw. ©1994 Dan Chu and Associates. Julian Messner, a division of Silver Burdett Press, NJ.

"A Geyser of Oil!" from SPINDLETOP by James A. Clark and Michel T. Halbouty. ©1952 James A. Clark and Michel T. Halbouty. Random House, NY.

"Songs of the Navajo" from AMERICAN INDIAN POETRY by George W. Cronyn. © renewed 1962 George W. Cronyn. Reprinted by permission of Mrs. George W. Cronyn.

From SPANISH PIONEERS OF THE SOUTHWEST by Joan Anderson. ©1989 Joan Anderson. E.P. Dutton, a division of NAL Penguin Inc., NY.

"Grand Canyon, East: From the Air" from REMEMBERING AND OTHER POEMS by Myra Cohn Livingston. ©1989 Myra Cohn Livingston. Margaret K. McElderry Books, Macmillan Publishing Company, NY.

"A Walk Through My Rainforest" from THE DISTANT TALKING DRUM by Isaac Olaleye. ©1995 Isaac Olaleye. Wordsong Boyds Mill Press, Inc., PA.

"A Mountain View" from FROM SUMMER TO SUMMER by Rose Burdunder. ©1965 Rose Styron. The Viking Press, Inc., NY.

Excerpts from DEAR WORLD: HOW CHILDREN AROUND THE WORLD FEEL ABOUT OUR ENVIRONMENT. Edited by Lannis Temple. ©1992. Random House Inc., NY.

Excerpt from THE DESERT IS THEIRS by Byrd Baylor. ©1975 by Byrd Baylor. Charles Scribner's Sons, NY.

## CREDITS

**Photography:** 20: Courtesy of Elio Reyes. 22: t.r. G. Anderson/The Stock market; b.l. Steve Elmore/The Stock Market. 23: t. l. Marmel Studios/The Stock Market. 48: t.r. Courtesy Penguin USA. 49: b. Courtesy NAACP Public Relations. 50: t. UPI/Bettman. 88: l. Rare Book Room/Detroit Public Library; r. MMSD. 89: Laura Ingalls Wilder Home Association; b. Courtesy of William Anderson Collection. 107: The Bettmann Archive. 126: NationalCowboy Hall of Fame. 153: Levi Strauss & Co.

**Cover:** Pentagram.

**Illustration:** Anthony Accardo 30, 149-151; Alex Bloch 46, 109; Elliott Banfield 38, 40; John Bowdren 54, 55; Bradford Brown 134; Michael Bryant 26; Circa 86, Inc. 58, 59; Judith Fast 14, 15, 16, 17; George Guzzi 75, 76, 99; Grace Goldberg 12, 103, 105, 145-148; James Grashow 132; Janet Hamlin 8-11, 142, 143, 154, 155, 159; Fiona King 2; Doug Knutson 67; Kelly Maddox 52; Anni Matsick 56; Jim McConnell 44, 90, 95; Marty Norman 63, 64; Rik Olson 78; Donna Perrone 27-29; Jan Pyk 24; Ernesto Ramos 116; Marcy Ramsey 162-165, 167; Joel Rodgers 120; Joanna Roy 84, 87, 117, 123, 126; Dennis Schofield 60, 62, 127, 130; Madeline Sorel 69, 70, 72, 74; Andrea Tachiera 136; M. Kathryn Thompson 144; Stefano Vitale 112-115;

**Text Design:** Circa 86, Inc.

# TEACHING Strategies

Teachers share a common goal—to help their students become successful learners who can understand, remember, and apply important knowledge and skills. This important goal is best supported when students are offered a variety of ways in which to learn.

The Social Studies Anthology offers you the rich and varied tools that you need to help your students learn. It includes such diverse sources as diaries, poems, songs, stories, legends, plays, and posters — all of which draw students into the sights and sounds of the places and times they are studying.

You may invite students to explore the Anthology selections in many unique ways— rewriting documents in another genre, dramatizing the selection, creating posters or collages, or writing original poems, stories, and songs. We have provided a strategy for teaching each selection in the Anthology. But these strategies, of course, are only suggestions. You should feel free to teach the selections in any way that you feel is best suited for your own classroom.

A Cassette accompanies the Social Studies Anthology and provides additional support in teaching the documents. Sometimes the recordings reproduce the voices of the people who wrote the selections. A Cassette logo lets you know which selections have been recorded.

# BRINGING THE PRAIRIE HOME

**by Patricia MacLachlan**
Pages 2–3

Use with Chapter 1, Lesson 1

## Objectives

☐ *Recognize that people's lives are influenced by geography.*

☐ *Identify why geographical place is important to Patricia MacLachlan.*

☐ *Write a diary entry about the place where you live.*

### Writing a Diary Entry

After students have read the selection, ask them to describe how the author uses different senses to record her impressions of the prairie. (Responses may include that MacLachlan mentions the smell of the the earth, the softness of flowers, the look of the skies.) Discuss with students how the prairie has influenced MacLachlan's life. (It gave her a sense of connecting with history. It made her think of the people who lived before her and would live after her.) Ask students: *How did MacLachlan decide to leave clues about herself?* (She wrote in a diary.) *What did MacLachlan carry with her to remind her of the place that changed her?* (a bag of prairie dirt) Discuss with students what happened when MacLachlan took a bag of prairie dirt to a fourth-grade class. (She discovered that the children also had strong feelings about place.)

Ask students to identify the geographical features of the place where they live. Volunteers may give examples of why the place where they live is important to them. Then guide students in writing a diary entry about their "place." Encourage students to use sensory details in their diary entries. You may also wish to ask students to bring in or draw an object that reminds them of their geographical place.

# STATES AND CAPITALS

**by Professor Rap**
Pages 4–7

Use with Chapter 1, Lesson 1, and Chapter 2, Lesson 4

## Objectives

☐ *Recognize that our country is made up of 50 states, each of which has its own capital.*

☐ *Identify how Professor Rap uses rhyming words to help students to remember the names of state capitals.*

☐ *Write a rap song about your classroom or school.*

### Writing Your Own Song

Play the song on the cassette for students and have them read along with the lyrics. Then ask volunteers to sing the song aloud. Students might enjoy singing the song in small groups.

Ask students to identify some of the words that rhyme with the names of state capitals. (*summery*, Montgomery; *snow*, Juneau; *ocean blue*, Honolulu; *vitamin C*, Tallahassee) Discuss the elements that make the song effective. (rhythm, rhyming words, refrain) Then have students work individually or in small groups to write a rap song about their classroom or their school.

Before students begin writing, have them brainstorm a list of rhyming words that they might use in their songs. Write the list on chart paper or on the chalkboard to help students get started. After students have completed their songs, have volunteers present them to the class. Students might enjoy making a recording of their songs.

# A WALK ACROSS AMERICA
by Peter Jenkins
Pages 8–11

*Use with Chapter 1, Lesson 2*

## Objectives

- ❑ *Identify the major landforms that are described in A Walk Across America.*
- ❑ *Recognize the enormous challenge that Peter Jenkins's walk across the country represented.*
- ❑ *Trace Peter Jenkins's route across the United States on a map.*

## Background Information

After students have read the selection by Peter Jenkins, remind them that the selection they have read described just one part of Jenkins's walk across the United States. Tell students that Jenkins's walk took him through the following states and cities in this order: New York; Pennsylvania; Washington, D.C.; Virginia; North Carolina; Tennessee; Georgia; Alabama (through Montgomery and then Mobile); Louisiana (through New Orleans); Texas (through Dallas up near the northwest corner of the state); New Mexico; Colorado; Utah (through Salt Lake City); Idaho (through Boise); and Oregon.

## Tracing a Route

Direct students attention to the map of United States landforms in *Regions* page G10. As you read out the names of the states and cities Jenkins passed through, have students trace Jenkins's route on their maps. Ask volunteers to name the different types of landforms found on Jenkins's route. (mountains, hills, plateaus, plains) Ask students which of these landforms were probably the most difficult for him to cross. (Mountains probably presented him with the most difficulty; other types of landforms may have been just as difficult in bad weather conditions.) Ask students why much of Jenkins's route passed through the southern half of the United States. (Jenkins probably chose to take the southern route because weather conditions would be less harsh during the winter.)

# DEAR WORLD
edited by Lannis Temple
Pages 12–13

*Use with Chapter 1, Lesson 3*

## Objectives

- ❑ *Recognize the desire of children all over the world for a clean environment.*
- ❑ *Identify the specific environmental concerns of the letter writers.*
- ❑ *Write a letter about our country's environment.*

## Background Information

Guide students to locate the geographical regions of Iran, Japan, and Siberia in their atlases (Middle East, Far East, Russia). Like our country, Iran and Siberia are rich in natural resources (Iran: gas, oil, emeralds; Siberia, a part of Russia: coal, diamonds, oil, trees, and fish). Japan also has rich fishing and is world renowned for its automobile and electronics manufacturing. Point out that in these countries the waste products from heavy industrialization can contribute to problems of pollution.

## Writing Your Own Letter

After students have read the letters of Sanae, Natasha, and Hamidreza, have them discuss the main concerns expressed by each writer. Ask them: *What does each writer love, fear, and dream about the environment?* You may wish to divide the class into three groups and assign a specific letter to each. Students can then discuss as a class or in smaller groups how they might like to respond to one of the letter writers. Ask students: *What would you like to tell this person about our country's enviroment?*

Have each student write a letter to Sanae, Natasha, or Hamidreza. The letters can respond to specific issues the *Dear World* writer raises and can express the student's own thoughts about our environment. Students may wish to ask questions about the letter writer's country and/or offer ideas about how children from all countries can work to improve the environment. Some students may also wish to illustrate their letters. After students have completed their letters, invite volunteers to read theirs to the class.

# 50 SIMPLE THINGS KIDS CAN DO TO SAVE THE EARTH
by John Javna and The EarthWorks Group
Pages 14–17

**Use with Chapter 1, Lesson 3**

## Objectives

- ❑ *List ways in which people waste energy or contribute to pollution.*
- ❑ *Identify how we can improve the environment through recycling and conservation.*
- ❑ *Participate in activities to improve the environment.*

## Building Citizenship

After students have read the selection, ask them to name the items mentioned that are important to recycle and conserve. List responses on chart paper or on the chalkboard. Ask students: *Which of these items are recyclable?* (glass) *Which of these items are not recyclable?* (Styrofoam products) *Which of these items are important to conserve?* (all)

Next have volunteers list on chart paper or the chalkboard ways in which people waste energy or contribute to pollution. Encourage students to suggest how they could waste less or conserve natural resources.

Divide the class into groups and have each group choose one conservation project—such as recycling glass, saving paper, or using less water. Have each group design a poster to publicize its project. If possible, have students display the posters in school hallways. Invite students to carry out their projects—for example, students could set up recycling centers.

Students might enjoy reading more of *50 Simple Things Kids Can Do to Save the Earth* or its sequel, *50 Simple Things Kids Can Do to Recycle*. They can look for these books in their school or local library.

# I HEAR AMERICA SINGING
by Walt Whitman
Page 18

# I, TOO
by Langston Hughes
Page 19

**Use with Chapter 2, Lesson 1**

## Objectives

- ❑ *Identify how Walt Whitman uses poetry to describe his view of America.*
- ❑ *Identify how Langston Hughes uses poetry to describe his hopes for African Americans.*
- ❑ *Write a poem linking both poems to America today.*

## Linking to Today

After students have read each poem, play the poems on the cassette. Share with students that they are hearing Langston Hughes read his own poem. After listening to the poems, volunteers might want to read the poems aloud to the class. Discuss with students the people and workers referred to in Whitman's poem. (mechanics, carpenter, mason, boatman, and so on) Ask students to identify the line in Hughes's poem that shows it was written in response to Whitman's. ("I, too, sing America.") Ask students why they think Hughes felt the need to write a response. (because Whitman had written about ordinary people, but not people who were sent to the kitchen to eat)

Have students listen again to the Hughes recording. Remind them that they are listening to Langston Hughes reading his own poem. Ask them to listen for a difference between the written and the recorded versions of the poem. (Hughes says, "They'll see how beautiful we are"; the poem is written, "They'll see how beautiful I am.") Ask students: *Why do you think Hughes changed the words? Which version do you prefer?*

Have students write a poem about America today. Encourage them to write about what they hear America singing. Students might enjoy illustrating their poems. After students have completed their poems, ask volunteers to read them to the rest of the class.

# BECOMING A CITIZEN
**Pages 20–21**

*Use with Chapter 2, Lessons 1 and 2*

## Objectives

❑ *Identify the process that immigrants must follow in order to become citizens of the United States.*

❑ *Recognize some of the difficulties faced by immigrants coming to the United States.*

❑ *Write questions to ask in an interview with a recent immigrant to the United States.*

## Writing an Interview

After students have read the selection, have them list some of the things that immigrants must do in order to obtain citizenship in the United States. (fill out application forms, take an oath of allegiance, interview with an Immigration and Naturalization Service official) Write responses on chart paper or on the chalkboard. Ask students: *What difficulties might new immigrants face as they apply for citizenship?* (problems with language, lack of money for fees) Why are people willing to go through such a difficult process in order to acquire United States citizenship? (Accept all reasonable answers.) You might wish to have students read and discuss the experiences of children immigrating to America in the early 1900s (pages 75–77).

If possible, arrange to have a recent immigrant or new citizen visit the class. Before the scheduled visit have students work in pairs to write questions for the interview. During the visit have one student in each pair ask the prepared questions and have the other write the answers. After the interview collect the questions and answers in a class book titled "Interviewing a New Immigrant" or "Interviewing a New Citizen." If possible, record the interview on a video or tape recorder.

# SYMBOLS OF THE NATION
**Pages 22–23**

*Use with Chapter 2, Lesson 2*

## Objectives

❑ *Explain how and why symbols are used to express ideas.*

❑ *Identify important symbols of the United States.*

❑ *Create symbols to represent your school or classroom.*

## Creating Symbols

Have students read the selection and examine the symbols. Then ask them why people use symbols. (as a sign to represent something, to communicate without language) Ask volunteers to describe other national symbols not mentioned in the selection. (Possible examples include Uncle Sam, the Lincoln Memorial, and the White House.)

Ask students to consider how they might use a symbol to represent their school or classroom. Have them work individually or in groups to design a symbol. Ask volunteers to write a brief description that explains their symbol. Then have them share their designs with the rest of the class. Display the symbols on the bulletin board.

# NEW COLOSSUS
by Emma Lazarus
Page 24 🎵

*Use with Chapter 2, Legacy*

## Objectives

- ❏ *Recognize some of the reasons that immigrants come to the United States.*
- ❏ *Identify how Emma Lazarus uses poetry to describe the significance of the Statue of Liberty.*
- ❏ *Write a poem or short essay from the perspective of an immigrant arriving in New York Harbor.*

### Rewriting from Another Perspective

After students have read the poem, play the recording on the cassette. Then ask a volunteer to read the poem aloud. Help students to understand difficult words or phrases.

Help students to understand that Emma Lazarus is presenting the statue's point of view in the line, "Keep, ancient lands, your storied pomp!" The statue's point of view is continued in the line, "I lift my lamp beside the golden door!"

Have students imagine that they are immigrants arriving by ship in New York Harbor. Ask them how they might describe the Statue of Liberty and their feelings toward it. Then have students write their own poem or a brief essay from an immigrant's point of view. Have students illustrate their writing. Encourage volunteers to share their writings and illustrations with the class.

# KNOXVILLE, TENNESSEE
by Nikki Giovanni
Page 26 🎵

*Use with Chapter 3, Lesson 2*

## Objectives

- ❏ *Recognize the reasons that the poet likes summer best of all the seasons.*
- ❏ *Identify how Nikki Giovanni uses poetry to describe what summer means to her.*
- ❏ *Write a poem about one of the seasons.*

### Writing Your Own Poem

After students have read the poem, play it for them on the cassette. After listening to the poem, volunteers might enjoy reading it aloud to the class. Discuss with students why they think Nikki Giovanni chose to write a poem about the summer. Have students suppose that the poem had no title. Ask students: *What elements from the poem might help you determine which region the poem is written about?* (fresh corn, okra, gospel music, mountains, warm climate year-round) Ask volunteers to tell which seasons are most special for them. Ask questions such as: *What do you like to do during your favorite season? How does the geography of our region affect the activities you do during each season?*

Then have students write poems about their favorite seasons and illustrate them. Make a bulletin-board display of the poems around the title "Our Favorite Seasons."

# WHEN I WAS YOUNG IN THE MOUNTAINS

by Cynthia Rylant
Pages 27–29

*Use with Chapter 3, Lesson 1*

## Objectives

❏ *Identify some of Cynthia Rylant's memories of living in the mountains.*

❏ *Describe how the use of repetition affects the story.*

❏ *Write a story about everyday life.*

### Writing Your Own Story

After students have read the selection, discuss with them the things that the author remembered about her everyday life as a child in the mountains. Have volunteers read aloud their favorite paragraphs from the selection. Then ask volunteers to tell about everyday things that were special to them when they were younger. Encourage students to think about their everyday lives and to compare them with the author's childhood memories.

Have students write a story called *When I Was Young in _____*. Suggest that students begin each paragraph with the phrase, "When I was young in _____." After students have completed their stories, invite volunteers to read them to the class.

# JOHN HENRY

**Traditional Ballad**
Pages 30–31 🔲

*Use with Chapter 3, Lesson 3*

## Objectives

❏ *Recognize that during the 1870s machines started to replace men in building railroads.*

❏ *Understand the origins of the folk hero John Henry and the story of how he challenged the machines.*

❏ *Write a new verse to the song "John Henry."*

### Writing Your Own Song Verse

After students have read the lyrics of the song, play Paul Robeson's performance of the ballad for them on the cassette. Point out to students that the written words differ from the words on the cassette. Tell them that this ballad is a traditional one with many variations. Have students compare the written verses with the cassette version. Ask: *Why do you think different versions became popular?* (The song was sung in many different parts of the country; over time people added their own verses.)

Divide the class into small groups and have each group write a new verse to "John Henry." After the new verses have been completed, make copies so that everyone can join in singing. If possible, record the class singing the song with old verses and new.

# IN COAL COUNTRY
## by Judith Hendershot
Pages 32–36

*Use with Chapter 3, Lesson 3*

## Objectives

- ❑ *Identify the way the story intermingles the good and bad features of life in Willow Grove.*
- ❑ *Identify the process of mining coal.*
- ❑ *Draw a storyboard with captions that explain family life in a coal-mining community.*

### Drawing Storyboards with Captions

After students have read the story, discuss what was good about life in Willow Grove and what was bad. (*good*: doing important work to be proud of, having lots of friends, sharing enjoyable times, celebrating Christmas; *bad*: hard work for adults, dirty water and air, noise from coal trains) Ask students: *Do you think that the children and parents felt the same way about life in Willow Grove? Why or why not?*

You might want to bring in some small pieces of coal and show them to students. Help students to break the pieces apart carefully with hammers. Have them discuss why coal mining is such dusty work.

Have small groups of students prepare storyboards for an imaginary video about life in Willow Grove. Divide the class into six groups. Ask each group of students to draw a scene that represents one of the parts of, or information from, the selection: 1. children's life in Willow Grove; 2. Papa's job in coal mining; 3. Mama's experiences with the family; 4. how coal was mined; 5. how coal was burned; 6. how coal was transported. Have students write captions for their storyboards. After students have completed their storyboards, display them on the bulletin board with the title "Life in a Coal-Mining Community."

# SEQUOYAH'S GIFT
## by Janet Klausner
Pages 37–40

*Use with Chapter 4, Lesson 1*

## Objectives

- ❑ *Explain why there was a need for Sequoyah's writing system.*
- ❑ *Identify how a syllabary works.*
- ❑ *Write about the new writing system from the perspective of someone in the selection.*

### Exploring Perspectives

After students have read the selection, ask volunteers to explain why Sequoyah wanted to invent a system of writing. (He wanted to preserve the Cherokee language and Cherokee customs.) Then ask: *How did Sequoyah's system of writing work?* (Make sure students understand that in Sequoyah's syllabary each symbol stands for a syllable.) Finally, discuss why Sequoyah's system was so important. (Because of it, the Cherokee were able to permanently record their history.)

Divide the class into four groups. Have each group represent one of the following people: 1. Sequoyah (before his system is accepted); 2. Sequoyah's daughter Ah-yo-kah (after she masters her father's system); 3. Town Chief Ah-gee-lee (before he witnesses Ah-yo-kah's performance); 4. Big Rattling Gourd (the night after he hears Sequoyah read in court).

Within their groups have students discuss the perspective of their assigned players toward the new writing system. Then continuing in groups, or individually, students can write a monologue from that person's point of view. Ask them to suppose someone has just asked them questions such as: *What is this Cherokee writing system I've been hearing about? Does it really work? Of what use is it?* After students have completed their monologues, have volunteers read theirs aloud to the other groups. Follow up with a class discussion about how and why the perspectives of these four people varied.

# JOHN GREENHOW'S STORE
**by Ron and Nancy Goor**
**Pages 41–42**

*Use with Chapter 4, Lesson 2*

## Objectives

- ❑ *Identify the ways colonists in Virginia paid for their goods.*
- ❑ *List and discuss items for sale in a general store in colonial Williamsburg.*
- ❑ *Write a response to the question "How was shopping in colonial times similar to and different from shopping today?"*

## Linking to Today

After students have read the selection, discuss the methods of buying and selling in colonial Virginia. Ask students: *How did colonists in Virginia pay for goods?* (ready money—Spanish or Dutch coins; notes of credit; barter) *What forms of payment were accepted in John Greenhow's store?* (ready money only) *Why couldn't colonists mint their own money?* (England would not allow it.) Have students look at the photograph of the store and name some of the goods for sale.

Then ask students to compare items available in Greenhow's store to items for sale in a store today. (Responses will vary but may include that many small stores today are more specialized.) Ask students what they think of as a "general store" today. (Accept all reasonable answers.) Have students write a short essay in response to the question "How was shopping in colonial times similar to and different from shopping today?" As a prewriting warm-up, students can make a list or Venn diagram of similarities and differences. When students have finished their essays, ask volunteers to read theirs to the class.

# THE BRAVE CONDUCTOR
**by Virginia Hamilton**
**Pages 43–45**

*Use with Chapter 4, Lesson 3*

## Objectives

- ❑ *Identify important events in the life of Harriet Tubman.*
- ❑ *Recognize that Virginia Hamilton condenses Tubman's biography while retaining its drama.*
- ❑ *Create a poster illustrating a period in Tubman's life.*

## Creating a Poster

After students have finished reading the selection, ask volunteers to share their reactions to Harriet Tubman's life story. You may wish to ask students: *How is this selection different from other stories you may have read about Harriet Tubman.* (Answers will vary but may include that Hamilton covers Tubman's entire life span.) Ask students why Tubman was called a "conductor." (She led people to freedom on the Underground Railroad.) Then ask them to name some of Harriet Tubman's other contributions to society (She served as a nurse during the Civil War, spoke out for the things she believed in, made her own house into a home for people in need.)

Have students draw posters illustrating different periods in Tubman's life. Divide the class into six groups and assign as topics: 1. Harriet's childhood in slavery; 2. running away; 3. reaching freedom; 4. speaking out at meetings (against slavery and for women's rights); 5. serving as a nurse in North Carolina; 6. keeping her home for people in need toward the end of her life. After students have completed their posters, display them in chronological sequence. Invite students to vote on a title for the poster display.

# BATTLE CRY OF FREEDOM

**Civil War Battle Songs**
**Pages 46–47** 🔲

*Use with Chapter 4, Lesson 3*

## Objectives

☐ *Identify the perspective revealed in the lyrics to the Northern version of the popular Civil War song "Battle Cry of Freedom."*

☐ *Identify the perspective revealed in the lyrics to the Southern version of "Battle Cry of Freedom."*

☐ *Write an essay about the different perspectives of the North and the South during the Civil War.*

## Exploring Perspectives

After students have read the lyrics, play the songs for them on the cassette. Ask volunteers to describe how the songs are alike. (same melody and harmony) Ask students: *How are they different?* (different lyrics) Have students find differences in the lyrics. (Union/Dixie; up with the star/up with the cross; and although he may be poor he shall never be a slave/their motto is resistance—"To tyrants we'll not yield!") Discuss the differences between the North and the South as expressed in the songs.

Have students write a short essay on the different perspectives that the people of the North and the people of the South had during the Civil War. After students have completed their essays, ask volunteers to read them to the class.

# ROSA PARKS: MY STORY

**by Rosa Parks**
**Pages 48–50**

*Use with Chapter 4, Lesson 4*

## Objectives

☐ *Recognize the importance of Rosa Parks's refusal to give up her seat on a bus.*

☐ *Identify how reading Rosa Parks's own words helps to better understand the event.*

☐ *Write a newspaper article about the event described in Rosa Parks: My Story.*

## Rewriting in Another Genre

After students have read the excerpt from *Rosa Parks: My Story*, have volunteers read the selection aloud. Ask students to identify the parts of the story that only Rosa Parks knows. (the many places where she describes her thoughts and feelings) Ask students why Rosa Parks finally wrote her own story about the events of December 1955. (probably to finally tell the details correctly)

Have students rewrite *Rosa Parks: My Story* as a newspaper article. Remind students of the "5 Ws"—the *who, what, when, where,* and *why*. Suggest that in their articles students "interview" the bus driver and other passengers on the bus. After students have completed their articles, ask volunteers to read them to the rest of the class.

# I SEE THE PROMISED LAND
**by Martin Luther King, Jr.**
**Page 51** 🔲

*Use with Chapter 4, Lesson 4*

## Objectives

❑ *Recognize the leadership of Martin Luther King, Jr., in the civil rights movement.*

❑ *Describe the effect of Dr. King's speech "I See the Promised Land."*

❑ *Write a response to the question, "Have we reached King's 'promised land'?"*

### Linking to Today

After students have read the speech, play it for them on the cassette. Tell students that they are listening to Martin Luther King, Jr., speaking his own words. Ask students to describe how King's words affected them. Discuss the difference between the effect of reading the speech and hearing it on the cassette. Ask students what King meant by the "promised land." (a place and time when racial harmony would be achieved)

Have students write a short essay in response to the question "Have we reached King's 'promised land'?" When students have completed their essays, ask volunteers to share them with the class.

# PUERTO RICO
**by Eileen Figueroa**
**Page 52** 🔲

*Use with Chapter 3, Lesson 1*

## Objectives

❑ *Recognize how Eileen Figueroa expresses her love for Puerto Rico through poetry.*

❑ *Write a poem about a special place.*

### Writing Your Own Poem

After students have read the poem, play it for them on the cassette. After listening to the poem in Spanish and English, volunteers might want to read aloud both versions to the class. Discuss with students why Eileen Figueroa might have chosen to express herself through poetry. (Poetry is often used to express beauty and emotion.) Ask students: *What special features of Puerto Rico does Figueroa describe?* (its beauty, its palm trees, its sea breezes) *How does she describe the evenings on the island?* (calming and serene with *coquíes*—little frogs— singing in the distance)

Ask volunteers to tell about a special place they know. Ask such questions as: *What about the place makes it special? Is it the sights? Is it the sounds? Is it the people?* Have students write their own poems about a special place. Students might enjoy illustrating their poems. Create a book of poems titled "Our Special Places."

# THE LONG TRAIL
by Monica Mayper
Page 54 🔲

---

*Use with Chapter 5, Lesson 1*

## Objectives

- ☐ *Identify how Monica Mayper uses poetry to describe a New England mountain trail.*
- ☐ *List the natural features described in the poem.*
- ☐ *Write a poem about a natural resource or place.*

### Writing Your Own Poem

After students have read the poem, play it for them on the cassette. Then ask a volunteer to read the poem aloud to the class. Discuss with students why Monica Mayper might have chosen to write a poem about a hike in the mountains. (Accept all reasonable answers.) Ask students: *What are some of the natural features Mayper describes?* (rock, creek-bed, birch, pine, plants, valley, and mountains) Discuss with students how the poet uses language to recreate the experience for the reader. (Lines like "on rock, on root, on rock" require pauses and are "hard to get around," just like rocks and roots on a mountain trail. The dramatic pause after "And then—" creates a sudden clearing on the page just as the speaker comes to a clearing on the path. The repetition of the word *mountains* in the last line creates a sense of mountains stretching out as far as the eye can see.)

Ask volunteers to tell about landforms or bodies of water in their own geographical region or in places they have visited. Ask students: *How does the geography of a region affect what people do there?* (Students might mention skiing or sledding on snow-covered hills, swimming in lakes or oceans, playing ball in a field, and so on.)

Have students write a poem about a natural place. Ask them to think about what kind of language would best describe the experience of being in that place. Allow students to brainstorm ideas in a group before writing the poem. After students have completed their poems, the poems can be illustrated, read aloud, and displayed in class.

# FALL
by Karla Kuskin
Page 55 🔲

---

*Use with Chapter 5, Lesson 2*

## Objectives

- ☐ *Identify images of autumn in the Northeast in Karla Kuskin's poem "Fall."*
- ☐ *Identify similarities and differences between "Fall" and the poem "The Long Trail" on page 54.*
- ☐ *Write a comparison of the two poems.*

### Writing a Comparison

After students have read the poem, play the recording on the cassette. Then ask volunteers to read the poem aloud. Have students describe some of the sensory images the poet uses. (Students might quote such lines as "I stop to watch the deer," "The black bears roar like thunder," or "I crunch through piles of…leaves.") Ask students: *If you could not see the title or first line, which parts of the poem would help you to determine which season the poem is about?* (chipmunks gathering butternuts, colorful hat and jacket, red and yellow leaves) *How does the time of year and climate affect people's activities?* (Answers will vary.)

Guide students in comparing this poem to "The Long Trail" on the facing page. Ask students: *How are the poems alike?* (Answers might include that both include images of the Northeast, both are about nature, both discuss enjoyable walks in wooded areas, both are in the first person.) Ask: *How are the poems different?* (Answers might include that "Fall" uses rhymes while "The Long Trail" is in free verse; "Fall" has shorter lines and "The Long Trail" longer; "The Long Trail" has more challenging vocabulary; "Fall" is a little more playful in tone, while the speaker in "The Long Trail" seems more in awe of the surrounding environment.)

After the group discussion have students write a short essay comparing the two poems. Volunteers can read their comparisons to the class.

# BLOW, YE WINDS, IN THE MORNING
Pages 56–57

*Use with Chapter 5, Lesson 3 and Legacy*

## Objectives

☐ *Explain why the Northeast was a rich whaling area.*

☐ *Identify how the song "Blow, Ye Winds, in the Morning" describes aspects of the whaling industry.*

☐ *Write additional verses to "Blow, Ye Winds, in the Morning."*

## Writing Your Own Song Verse

After students have read the lyrics to the song, play it for them on the cassette. Then play the song again and invite the class to sing along as sailors on a whaling ship. Discuss with students why sailors might have made up such a song. (to pass time and amuse themselves on long trips) Have students identify other things mentioned in the song associated with the Northeast and the whaling industry. (New Bedford, whaling ports, clipper ships, running gear) Ask students: *What example of exaggeration can you find in this song?* (hunting 500 whales in six months) *Why do you think the whalers exaggerated?* (to get sailors to work on their ships)

Divide the class into small groups and have each group write one new verse to the song. Encourage students to think of experiences whalers might have while harvesting the sea. Remind students to pay attention to the use of exaggeration and the repetition of the words *out—singin'* in the verses' fourth lines. After the verses have been completed, copy song sheets for "hearty" classmates to sing and enjoy. The illustrated songs can become part of a sea-theme bulletin board. Students might wish to record their sailing songs.

# THE WALUM OLUM
by the Lenape-Algonkian People, 1700s
Pages 58–59

*Use with Chapter 6, Lesson 1*

## Objectives

☐ *Understand that the Lenape-Algonkian handed down their creation story from generation to generation through storytelling.*

☐ *Recognize that during the 1700s the Lenape-Algonkian first wrote* The Walum Olum *in pictographs.*

☐ *Write a story using pictographs.*

## Creating Your Own Pictographs

After students have read the selection and looked at the drawings, discuss why the Lenape-Algonkian used pictographs to write *The Walum Olum*. (They did not use an alphabet with letter symbols.) Ask students: *How do pictographs differ from other illustrations?* (Pictographs are simple line drawings.) Have students look closely at the pictographs to see if they can recognize what each symbol represents. Help students to recognize the sun, the crescent moon, the stars, and some of the animals in the pictographs.

Ask students to choose a folk tale that they know well—for example, one about Paul Bunyan, Johnny Appleseed, or Little Red Riding Hood. Discuss with students the characters and the story lines of several folk tales. Then have students draw pictographs to represent the most important scenes in the story. Or students might choose to draw scenes from a story they make up themselves. Display the completed pictographs on the bulletin board.

# TURTLE'S RACE WITH BEAR

**An Iroquois Tale Retold by Joseph Bruchac**
**Pages 60–62**

*Use with Chapter 6, Lesson 1*

## Objectives

- ❏ *Recognize that cooperation was important to the people of the Iroquois Confederacy.*
- ❏ *Explain how Turtle's Race with Bear teaches the value of teamwork.*
- ❏ *Perform Turtle's Race with Bear as Readers Theater.*

## Using Readers Theater

After students have read the selection, discuss it with them. Ask students: *How is Turtle able to win the race against Bear?* (by enlisting the help of other turtles) Discuss what the turtles' action shares with the founding of the Iroquois Confederacy. (The turtles join together to defeat Bear; the five groups of the Iroquois joined together to be strong against outsiders.) Ask: *What does this story teach?* (Answers may vary, but will probably include the importance of cooperation.)

Ask students whether they think Turtle's victory was fair. (Answers will vary.) Explain to students that "trickster" figures are common to the folk tales of many different cultures. You may wish to ask students whether they know of any other tales where a clever character tricks someone who has wronged him or her. Invite volunteers to share stories they know with the class.

Have students perform *Turtle's Race with Bear* as Readers Theater. Remind students that in Readers Theater they do not move about but try to read with expression. Choose volunteers to play the roles of Turtle and Bear. Choose another student as Narrator and have him or her read the descriptive parts of the selection. If you wish, you can divide the text into three parts and assign different actors for each part. Encourage students to familiarize themselves with their lines before the performance. Students who are not playing roles may wish to make drawings of scenes or characters from the story. These can be displayed as a backdrop for the reading.

# PAUL REVERE'S RIDE

**by Henry Wadsworth Longfellow**
**Pages 63–66** 🔊

*Use with Chapter 6, Lesson 2*

## Objectives

- ❏ *Recognize the importance of Paul Revere's ride to the American Revolution.*
- ❏ *Identify how Longfellow uses language to dramatize the story of Revere's ride.*
- ❏ *Rewrite the poem as a newspaper article.*

## Rewriting in Another Genre

After students have read the poem, play the recording on the cassette. Then either invite volunteers to read verses of the poem or have the class do a choral reading of the poem. Ask students: *Why was Paul Revere's ride important?* (Because of his warning, Americans had time to prepare for a British attack.) After each section of the poem is read, ask students to summarize the *who, what, when, where,* and *why* of the story. The responses can be recorded on chart paper or on the chalkboard. Encourage students to make notes on these summaries, which they can include in a time line of Revere's ride.

Guide students working individually, in pairs, or in small groups, to rewrite the poem as a newspaper article. First have students review their summaries of the poem's sections. Before they start their newspaper articles, remind students of the "5 Ws"—the *who, what, where, when,* and *why.* After students have completed their articles, ask volunteers to read theirs to the rest of the class.

# HARD TIMES AT VALLEY FORGE

**by Joseph Martin, 1777–1778**
**Pages 67–68**

*Use with Chapter 6, Lesson 2*

## Objectives

- ☐ *Describe the hardships faced by the soldiers at Valley Forge as described in Joseph Martin's diary.*
- ☐ *Identify the reasons that Joseph Martin remained in the army despite the hardships.*
- ☐ *Rewrite Joseph Martin's diary entry as a newspaper article.*

## Rewriting in Another Genre

Have students share in reading this selection aloud. After the selection has been read, discuss with students the hardships described by Joseph Martin. (lack of food, water, clothing, and shelter; fatigue; freezing temperatures) Ask students which of Joseph Martin's experiences they consider to have been the most difficult. Have students look again at the selection to find a sentence in his diary that explains why Martin may have been willing to undergo such extreme hardship. (Martin wrote: "We had engaged in the defense of our injured country and were willing, nay, we were determined to persevere as long as such hardships were not altogether intolerable....") Ask students why Joseph Martin might have decided to keep a diary during this difficult experience. (to stave off boredom, to relieve loneliness, to help him remember the period in his life after the war was over)

Have students rewrite *Hard Times at Valley Forge* as a newspaper article. Remind students of the "5 Ws"—the *who, what, when, where,* and *why.* After students have completed their articles, have volunteers read them aloud to the class.

# IN THE YEAR OF THE BOAR AND JACKIE ROBINSON

**by Bette Bao Lord**
**Pages 69–74**

*Use with Chapter 6, Lesson 3*

## Objectives

- ☐ *Identify the difficulties faced by new immigrants like Shirley Temple Wong.*
- ☐ *Recognize that despite the problems they confront, many people still choose to immigrate to the United States.*

## Background Information

Help students to understand that the phrase "year of the boar" refers to the Chinese calendar. Each of the 12 years of the Chinese calendar is referred to by a different animal name: rat, ox, tiger, hare, dragon, snake, horse, sheep, monkey, rooster, dog, and pig (or boar). The year 1947 was the year of the boar.

## Linking to Today

After students have read the selection, ask them to list the difficulties that Shirley Temple Wong experienced in her first year in the United States. (language problems, teasing from her classmates for being the "teacher's pet," unfamiliarity with American customs) Discuss with students the connection between Shirley Temple Wong and Jackie Robinson. (Robinson overcame hostility and injustice to excel and make a change. He became a hero to Wong, who felt isolated and confused in her adopted culture.)

Students should realize that although the story about Shirley Temple Wong takes place in 1947, it describes problems faced by immigrants today. Have students write a paragraph explaining why many immigrants find it worthwhile to face these challenges. Ask volunteers to share their responses with the class.

# I WAS DREAMING TO COME TO AMERICA

Memories from the Ellis Island Oral History
Project Selected by Veronica Lawlor
Pages 75–77

*Use with Chapter 6, Lesson 3*

## Objectives

❑ *Describe the experiences of six people who immigrated to America in the early 1900s.*

❑ *Identify the different reasons people have for coming to this country.*

❑ *Trace the immigration route of the immigrants in the selection.*

## Background Information

After students have read the selection, you may wish to share with them some additional biographical facts from the book *I Was Dreaming to Come to America* about the people interviewed. Golda Meir is a name students may have heard. Meir went on to serve as Prime Minister of Israel from 1969–1974. Vartan Hartunian graduated with honors from a Northeastern college and became a minister, like his father. Edward Corsi continued his involvement with Ellis Island, becoming its commissioner of immigration in 1931. Brigitta Hedman Fichter eventually settled in New Jersey and became a real-estate agent. Visitors to the immigration museum on Ellis Island can see her mother's shoes on display. Lazarus Salamon came to this country with only a brother and sister. The family of siblings settled in New York, and Lazarus eventually became a salesperson. Helen Cohen also worked as a salesperson, but in Washington, D.C. She and her Russian-born husband had twin girls in 1925.

## Tracing a Route

Discuss with students the speakers' reasons for immigrating and their impressions of their new homeland. Working in small groups, students can refer to their atlases and trace the routes that each immigrant may have taken from his or her country to Ellis Island.

# CITY, CITY

by Marci Ridlon
Page 78 🎵

*Use with Chapter 6, Lesson 4*

## Objectives

❑ *List the good things and the bad things about living in a city that are mentioned in this selection.*

❑ *Recognize that there are both good and bad things about living in most places.*

❑ *Write a poem describing some of the good and the bad things about living in your own community.*

## Writing Your Own Poem

After students have read the poem, play it for them on the cassette. After students have listened to the poem, ask volunteers to read it aloud. Discuss with students why the poet might have chosen to write the poem in two columns, side by side.

Ask volunteers to describe some of the things they like about their community. Then ask them to describe some of the things they dislike. Have students write their own poems about their communities. Suggest that they also write a poem in two columns. Have students illustrate their poems. Then ask volunteers to share their poems and illustrations with the class.

# HEARTLAND
**by Diane Siebert**
**Pages 80–83**

*Use with Chapter 7, Lesson 1*

## Objectives

❑ *Recognize why Diane Siebert calls the Middle West the "heartland."*

❑ *Identify how Diane Siebert uses poetry to celebrate the farmers and their land.*

❑ *Write a poem about your own region.*

## Writing Your Own Poem

After students have read the poem, play it for them on the cassette. After they have listened to the poem, ask volunteers to read it aloud. Discuss with students why they think that Diane Siebert uses the word *heartland* to describe the Middle West. (because the region produces much of the food that feeds the people of the United States; because the Middle West is geographically at the center of, or at the heart of, the United States; because the heart feeds blood to the body.) Have students imagine that the poem has no title. Ask students: *How would you identify the region that this poem describes?* (fields of grain, blizzards, giant mills, stockyards, wheat fields, cornfields, and the many references to farms and farmers) Have volunteers share features of their own region that make it special. Encourage students to brainstorm about their region. As students name examples, list them on chart paper or on the chalkboard.

Have each student write a poem about his or her region. Encourage students to think about the entire region and the changes that occur with the different seasons of the year. After students have completed their poems, have them draw illustrations to accompany them. Encourage volunteers to share their poems and illustrations with the class.

# SKYLARK
**by Patricia MacLachlan**
**Pages 84–87**

*Use with Chapter 7, Lesson 2, and Chapter 8, Lesson 1*

## Objectives

❑ *Identify how a drought threatens a Middle West farm family in the novel* Skylark.

❑ *Describe how Sarah and her family react to the drought.*

❑ *Perform* Skylark *as Readers Theater.*

## Using Readers Theater

After students have read the selection, discuss it with them. Ask students: *How did the temperature affect Sarah's family in the summer?* (Without rain, the intense heat produced a drought and a dry river. Sarah and the children had to return to Maine.) Have students discuss the meaning of the novel's title. (Maggie refers to Sarah as a prairie lark—it sings a song in the sky before making its home on land.) Have students compare their region's climate with the hot summers and cold winters of the Middle West prairie region as depicted in the novel.

Have students perform the selection as Readers Theater. Choose volunteers to play the parts of the main characters—Sarah, Caleb, Papa, Maggie, Matthew, and Anna. If need be, the parts can be double-cast. Several students can play farmers, friends of Sarah and her family. The student playing Anna can be the narrator, as she is in the selection, and can read the descriptive parts of the selection. Encourage students to practice saying their lines before the performance.

Students might enjoy reading all of *Skylark*. They may also wish to reread Patricia MacLachlan's essay *Bringing the Prairie Home* (pages 2–3).

# LIFE ON THE PRAIRIE
## with Laura Ingalls Wilder
Pages 88–89

*Use with Chapter 7, Lesson 2, and Chapter 8, Lesson 1*

## Objectives

- ❏ *Identify the objects from Laura Ingalls Wilder's life on the prairie.*
- ❏ *Recognize the importance of objects from the past.*
- ❏ *Create a montage of objects from students' lives.*

## Creating a Montage

After students have looked at the artifacts, discuss the value of seeing real objects from the past. Ask students: *Why is it interesting to look at the original manuscript, the photograph, and the old newspaper?* (The objects help us to feel a connection with the author.)

Have students work together in groups to create a montage of objects from their own lives. Suggest that each group choose three objects that represent students' lives. Have them title the montage "Life in [student's town]." When students have completed the montage, display it on the bulletin board.

# A BOY NAMED ABE
## by Susan Nanus
Pages 90–98

*Use with Chapter 8, Lesson 1*

## Objectives

- ❏ *Identify the strengths Abe Lincoln demonstrated as a boy growing up in Kentucky.*
- ❏ *Describe how scenes in the play* A Boy Named Abe *show those strengths.*
- ❏ *Write an additional scene for the play.*

## Writing Your Own Scene

After students have taken turns reading the play aloud, ask them to tell what they have learned about the character of Lincoln as a young boy growing up in Kentucky. (Responses might include comments about Abe's love of reading and how reading helped him; his hardworking and honest nature; his qualities of common sense, determination, and sense of humor.) You may wish to have students perform some scenes or all of the play.

Divide the class into four or five groups. Guide each group to do research in the library to find additional information about young Lincoln that could be the basis for a short scene. Suggest to students that they try to incorporate references to the woods, rivers, and other geographical features of Kentucky in their scenery. Have each group write a scene and read or perform it in the classroom.

# GOING HOME TO NICODEMUS
**by Daniel Chu and Bill Shaw**
**Pages 99–102**

*Use with Chapter 8, Legacy*

## Objectives

❑ *Recognize why, in 1878, freed blacks from Kentucky expected Kansas to be a "Promised Land."*

❑ *Describe what the freed black homesteaders really found in Nicodemus, Kansas.*

❑ *Create a mural showing the expectations, initial disappointment, and fulfilled dreams of the black homesteaders in Kansas.*

## Creating a Mural

After students have read the selection, discuss with them the expectations the freed black homesteaders in Kentucky had about traveling to Kansas. (After years of slavery, they were thrilled about the possibility of owning their own land and living as free people.) Have students describe the hardships the members of Reverend Hickman's church endured on their journey to Kansas. Then ask students: *What did the freed men and women actually find in Nicodemus, Kansas?* (Instead of a Promised Land they found settlers living in holes in the ground.) Discuss with students how the black homesteaders took their deep disappointment. (Many stayed on, and with great faith, built up Nicodemus as a thriving all-black frontier town in the Great Plains.)

Divide students into three groups covering these phases: freed black homesteaders' hard journey to Kansas, looking forward to the Promised Land; their disappointment on finding a desolate area without any comforts; and the all-black frontier town years later, with businesses, schools, and places of worship and recreation. Guide the three groups to create a three-part mural with the title "The Pioneering Spirit: Going Home to Nicodemus."

Students might enjoy reading all of *Going Home to Nicodemus*, which they may be able to find in their school or local library.

# THE BUFFALO GO
**by Old Lady Horse**
**Pages 103–104**

# BUFFALO DUSK
**by Carl Sandburg**
**Page 105** 🔊

*Use with Chapter 8, Lesson 2*

## Objectives

❑ *Recognize how the legend makes clear the importance of the buffalo to the Kiowa.*

❑ *Recognize how Carl Sandburg expresses through poetry his sadness over the loss of the buffalo.*

❑ *Compare and contrast the perspectives of the Kiowa and the hunters.*

## Exploring Perspectives

After students have read the legend and the poem, play the poem for them on the cassette. Tell students that they are listening to Carl Sandburg reading his own poem. Then discuss the selections with them. Ask volunteers to describe the reasons that the buffalo were important to the Kiowa. (They were sacrificed in the Sun Dance and used in the Kiowa's prayers; hides were used to make clothing and tepees; meat was used for food; bladders and stomachs were made into containers.) Ask students: *How did the buffalo become nearly extinct?* (Too many were killed.) *Why did some white settlers kill the buffalo?* (to make room for railroads, farms, and ranches; to sell the hides; to force the Indians onto reservations)

Have students discuss the different perspectives of the Kiowa and some white settlers toward the buffalo. Ask students: *Do you think that the perspective of the white hunters might be different today?* (Probably; because today there is more understanding and respect for other cultures.) Have students consider Carl Sandburg's perspective toward the buffalo. Point out that Sandburg was a European American who was saddened by the loss of the buffalo.

Have students write a short essay on the different perspectives of the Kiowa and some white settlers during the late 1800s. After students have completed their essays, ask volunteers to read them aloud.

# THE WABASH CANNONBALL
by A. P. Carter
Page 106 ▣

Use with Chapter 8, Lesson 3

## Objectives

❑ *Identify the significance of the song "The Wabash Cannonball."*

❑ *Create a poster about the Wabash Cannonball.*

## Creating Posters

After students have read the lyrics to the song, play it for them on the cassette. Ask students: *Why do you think that the train was called the Cannonball?* (because it rumbled, roared, and echoed down the valley like a cannonball) *Where did the Wabash Cannonball travel?* (from California to Labrador, with stops in St. Paul, Kansas City, Des Moines, and Kankakee) Help students to locate Labrador on a map of Canada. Have students trace the route on a map of the United States.

Have students draw posters to encourage people to ride the Wabash Cannonball. Encourage students to use images from the song for their posters. After students have completed their posters, display them on the bulletin board.

# DOTY'S WASHER
Advertisement from the 1800s
Page 107

# HITTING THE ROAD
Automobile Advertisements, 1902 and 1924
Page 108

Use with Chapter 8, Lesson 3

## Objectives

❑ *Recognize why housekeepers in the 1800s would prefer Doty's Washer to the old washboard.*

❑ *Compare automobile advertisements.*

❑ *Create a poster for a new product that will improve people's lives.*

## Creating a Poster

After students have read the introductory material for the two selections, discuss the information with them. Then guide students to look at the advertisements and posters and discuss why these products would have appealed to their intended audience. (Doty's Washer promised to "save their money and clothes" while reducing their work; the automobile created more jobs and provided easier transporation.) Have students discuss what they like and dislike about the washer and the automobiles in the advertisements.

Have students create a poster showing an advertisement for a product of their choice. Suggest that students show an advertisement for today on the left side of the poster. On the right side of the poster, have students draw an advertisement for the future. Have students write advertising copy describing the products. Display the completed advertisements on the bulletin board.

# WORKING THE LAND
**by Pierce Walker**
**Pages 109–110**

*Use with Chapter 8, Lesson 4*

### Objectives
- ❏ *Describe the life of Pierce Walker working on Indiana farms.*
- ❏ *Identify how farm life in Indiana has changed for Walker through the years.*
- ❏ *Write questions to ask in an interview with a farmer.*

### Writing an Interview

After students have read the selection, discuss it with them. Ask why Walker thinks farming is such a gamble and hard work. (dependency on weather, rising prices, long hours) Ask students: *What are some of the changes in farming Walker has experienced over the years?* (farming becoming big business; management problems; changing technology) Ask students: *If working on a farm is so hard for Walker and his family, why have they continued to farm?* (the pride of producing good crops, pride in work, often good to be by yourself in the fields)

If possible, arrange to visit a farm or have a farmer visit the class. Have students work in pairs to write questions for the interview. Guide one student in each pair to write down the question; the other student, the answer. Gather the questions and answers in a class book called "Working the Land." You might wish to have groups illustrate the cover and inside contents.

# KATE HEADS WEST
**by Pat Brisson**
**Pages 112–115**

*Use with Chapter 9, Lesson 1*

### Objectives
- ❏ *Identify some of the geographical attractions found in the Southwest as described in the selection.*
- ❏ *Draw postcards illustrating attractions of the Southwest.*

### Drawing Your Own Postcards

After students have read the selection, discuss each postcard with them. Ask students to imagine what picture might be shown on the first postcard. (a rodeo in Fort Worth) Suggest that students skim the message on the first postcard to find clues about the picture. Then ask students: *What pictures might be on the other postcards?* (the desert, the Rio Grande or Juarez, Gila Cliff Dwellings National Monument, the Petrified Forest, the Grand Canyon)

Divide the class into six groups. Have each group draw one postcard. Suggest that students reread Kate's message for possible images to use in their illustrations. After students have completed their postcards, display them on a bulletin board titled "Postcards from the Southwest."

# THE ERRAND
by Harry Behn
Page 116 🔲

*Use with Chapter 9, Lessons 1 and 2*

## Objectives

- ❏ *Identify some of the geographical features of the Southwest region of the United States.*
- ❏ *Recognize why Harry Behn described his errand through poetry.*
- ❏ *Draw a storyboard with captions for a video.*

### Drawing Storyboards with Captions

After students have read the poem, play it for them on the cassette. After listening to the poem, volunteers might want to read it aloud to the class. Direct students' attention to the different images described in each of the verses. (a trip by pony to a faraway farm, a water tank on top of a hill, a windmill bringing up rusty water, a graveyard overgrown with gourds and grass, a valley with one house and one tree, a book left inside an empty house, the setting sun and the rising moon) Ask volunteers to tell why they think Harry Behn chose to write about his errand in the form of a poem. (The journey to the neighboring farm was full of visual surprises; the poet is sensitive to beauty.)

Divide the class into seven groups, one for each of the poem's verses. Have one group draw a storyboard for each verse to plan a video of the poem. Then have each group write a caption for its storyboard. After the storyboards have been completed, display them on the bulletin board.

# THE DESERT IS THEIRS
by Byrd Baylor
Pages 117–119 🔲

*Use with Chapter 9, Lesson 2*

## Objectives

- ❏ *Describe how the Papago—the Desert People of the Southwest—are depicted in the poem.*
- ❏ *Recognize what Southwestern desert people, animals, and plants, share in common.*
- ❏ *Write a poem about the Southwestern desert.*

### Writing Your Own Poem

After students have read the poem, play it for them on the cassette. Have students take turns saying the lines in choral unison. Discuss with students how the desert people are described in the poem. (Accept all reasonable responses; record some on chart paper or on the chalkboard.) Ask students to list some things that, according to the poem, connect people, animals, and plants in the Southwestern desert. (living in harmony with nature, feelings of connection, sharing hard times and times of plenty, and so on)

Have students discuss their thoughts about the Southwestern desert. Students can work individually, in pairs, or in groups. Encourage students to compare their own climate with that of the desert. After they have completed their poems, students may wish to illustrate them. Display poems in a "Scrapbook of the Southwest" or on the bulletin board.

# A GEYSER OF OIL
**by James A. Clark and Michael T. Halbouty**
**Pages 120–122**

*Use with Chapter 9, Lesson 3*

## Objectives

- ❏ *Identify what a geyser is and what it does.*
- ❏ *Describe how drillers struck oil in Beaumont, Texas, in 1901.*
- ❏ *Conduct a "press conference" with the workers and townspeople who were involved in the oil strike.*

## Conduct a Press Conference

After students have read the selection, write the word *geyser* on the chalkboard and guide students in making associations with other words and ideas. (Students may suggest other kinds of geysers, or other oil well images.) Next have students take turns summarizing the steps in drilling for oil. (These can be listed on the chalkboard.) Have students describe the emotional reactions of Al and Curt Hamill, Peck Byrd, Louie Mayer, Charley Ingals, Patillo Higgins, and Captain Anthony Lucas to the discovery of oil. Discuss how the town of Beaumont changed after the oil strike. (Many became rich; the oil industry boomed.)

Have students write notes on one side of a 5 × 8 card about the people involved in the discovery of "black gold" gushing from Spindletop. On the other side of the note card, students can write notes and draw diagrams of the oil drilling process. Have students prepare questions for a press conference in which people connected with the Beaumont oil discovery are interviewed by student reporters covering the story. Drawings, replicas of "black gold," and diagrams of drilling can decorate the press conference room.

# PUEBLO STORYTELLER
**by Diane Hoyt-Goldsmith**
**Pages 123–125**

*Use with Chapter 10, Lesson 1*

## Objectives

- ❏ *Recognize that storytelling is an important tradition among the Pueblo people.*
- ❏ *Recognize how April has become a storyteller.*
- ❏ *Perform "How the People Came to Earth" as Readers Theater.*

## Using Readers Theater

After students have read the selection, discuss it with them. Ask students to name some of the subjects of the stories that April's grandparents told her. (legends of the Pueblo people, things that happened in their own lives) Ask students: *Which time of year was the subject of the story that was told to April by her grandmother?* (autumn) *What activities was the family involved in during autumn?* (harvesting and husking corn) *Which legend did April's grandparents tell her?* ("How the People Came to Earth")

Have students perform the selection as Readers Theater. Remind students that in a Readers Theater performance, the actors do not move around on a stage, but remain seated and use only their voices as a means to act out the dialogue. Choose students for the parts of the narrator, the mole, and Old Spider Woman. Several students can represent the people. Encourage students to familiarize themselves with the story before staging the performance.

# SONGS OF THE NAVAJO
excerpted from translations
by George W. Cronyn
Page 126 🔲

---

*Use with Chapter 10, Lesson 1*

## Objectives

- ❑ *Recognize how the Navajo's respect for nature is expressed in the poem.*
- ❑ *Identify how the poem connects seasons, as well as youth and old age.*
- ❑ *Write your own song that shows respect for nature and people.*

### Writing Your Own Poem

After students have read the poem, play it for them on the cassette. Ask students for examples of how the Navajo's respect for nature is expressed. (Almost every line is an example.) Have students identify the images that refer to seasons and to youth and old age. Lead a discussion about the poem's use of such devices as rhythm, repetition of words, and refrain. Have students write their own versions of a chant modeled after this one. Divide the class into groups. Have each group come up with a different refrain, such as "with patience may I grow" or "with light may I understand." Have students within these groups use their refrain to write individual poems. Encourage students to use poetic images associated with the beauty of the Southwest or with their own region.

# SPANISH PIONEERS OF THE SOUTHWEST
by Joan Anderson
Pages 127–130

---

*Use with Chapter 10, Lesson 2*

## Objectives

- ❑ *Recognize how early Spanish settlers lived in the Southwest.*
- ❑ *Describe how, after working hard on the farm, Miguel celebrated the Feast of San Ysidro (arrival of spring).*
- ❑ *Write a description of a ceremony.*

### Writing About a Ceremony

After students have read the selection, have them discuss life on the Baca family farm in the mid-1700s. Ask them: *What is Pedro Baca worried about?* (His older brother was taken by Navajo in a raid.) Discuss with students the importance of farming for the Baca family. Ask students: *What does Pedro look forward to?* (the Feast of San Ysidro) Discuss why this holiday was important for the Spanish farmers, and how they celebrated it. (It marked the arrival of spring; farmers receive blessings for the land; there was a procession with Saint Ysidro's statue; there was special food; there was a church ceremony.) Ask students how the Bacas felt about their Pueblo Indian neighbors. (shared appreciation and caring for the land) You might wish to record student responses on the chalkboard.

Ask volunteers to describe ceremonies they know about that celebrate a particular season or event. Then have students write a description of a ceremony. Some students may wish to make up their own ceremony. After students have completed their descriptions, ask volunteers to read them aloud in class. Students may wish to illustrate their written descriptions for display in the classroom.

# BILL PICKETT
**Cowboy Movie Poster**
**Page 131**

*Use with Chapter 10, Lesson 3*

## Objectives

❑ *Identify rodeo cowboys as public personalities.*

❑ *Identify the different elements of a movie poster.*

❑ *Create a new movie poster.*

## Linking to Today

Have students read about Bill Pickett. Ask: *Why do you think Bill Pickett was an unusual rodeo star?* (Responses will vary, but might include the fact that he was part Choctaw Indian.) Then have students examine the cowboy movie poster. Ask: *What information does this poster include?* (the name of the star, what he does in the movie, some language meant to sell the movie —"Thrills! Laughs too!" — the name of the film company, and the place the film was produced) Ask: *How do modern movie posters differ from this poster?* (Responses may vary, but should include the fact that today's movie posters are more glamorous and exciting, and reflect the kinds of movies being made today.)

Have students form small groups. Ask each group to come up with the name of a modern movie (a cowboy movie, if possible) and to create a poster advertising that movie. Display the finished posters on the bulletin board.

# GIT ALONG, LITTLE DOGIES
**Cowboy Song**
**Pages 132–133** 📼

*Use with Chapter 10, Lesson 3*

## Objectives

❑ *Understand why cowboys sang songs on cattle drives.*

❑ *Write a new verse to the song "Git Along, Little Dogies."*

## Writing a Song Verse

After students have read the lyrics to the song, play it for them on the cassette. Point out to students that the written words differ from the words on the cassette. Tell them that the song is a traditional one with many variations. Discuss with students why cowboys might have sung on the cattle drives. (to pass the time, to entertain themselves) Remind students that cowboys worked day after day, eating and sleeping outdoors. Ask students what the word dogies refers to in the song. (motherless or stray calves) Ask: *Why do you think the cowboys sometimes sang to the cattle and the dogies?* (as a way of talking to them)

Have students write a fourth verse to the song. Remind students to try to use rhyming words at the ends of the second and fourth lines. When students have completed their verses, have them draw accompanying illustrations. Encourage volunteers to share their verses and illustrations with the class.

# THE TEXAS SPIRIT
by Barbara Jordan
Pages 134–135

Use with Chapter 10, Lesson 4

## Objectives

❑ *Identify important events in Barbara Jordan's life as described in the interview.*

❑ *Recognize some of Barbara Jordan's personal strengths.*

❑ *Write an essay about Barbara Jordan.*

## Writing an Essay

After students have read the interview with Barbara Jordan, discuss the selection. Ask volunteers to share their reactions to Jordan's life as described in the interview. Encourage students to talk about Jordan's response to the obstacles she met. (She decided to change things.) Ask a volunteer to read aloud the paragraph that describes what Jordan's father taught her. Finally, ask a volunteer to read aloud what Jordan says about Texas.

Have students reread the selection and write a few sentences that summarize each paragraph. Tell students to use their sentences as a guideline for a brief essay about Barbara Jordan. After students have completed their essays, have volunteers read them to the class.

# GRAND CANYON EAST: FROM THE AIR
by Myra Cohn Livingston
Page 136 📼

Use with Chapter 9, Lesson 1

## Objectives

❑ *Identify the perspective the poet uses to describe the Grand Canyon.*

❑ *Identify the perspective the poet uses to compare the Grand Canyon with other objects.*

❑ *Write a new version of the poem from a different perspective.*

## Exploring Perspectives

After students have read the poem, play it for them on the cassette. Ask volunteers to identify the vantage point from which the Grand Canyon is described. (from high above) Next ask students to discuss what the poet compares the Grand Canyon to. (old apartment buildings) Ask students: *What do you think of this comparison?* (Responses will vary.)

Have students write their own versions of the poem from different perspectives of viewing the Grand Canyon. Suggestions might include: from the ground, from the inside, from the point of view of a rock or river, compared to another natural phenomenon, or compared to an object in the students' own geographical region. Display the poems, perhaps illustrated, in a canyonlike formation on the bulletin board. Encourage students to read their poems aloud or, if possible, record them for a class tape of student readings.

# SIERRA
**by Diane Siebert**
**Pages 138–141** 📼

*Use with Chapter 11, Lesson 1*

## Objectives

❏ *Recognize how Diane Siebert uses poetry to describe the history of the Sierra Mountains.*

❏ *Recognize some of the changes in the history of the Sierra Mountains.*

❏ *Write a letter to Diane Siebert.*

## Writing a Letter

After students have read the poem silently, play it for them on the cassette. Then ask volunteers to read the poem aloud. Discuss with students why Diane Siebert might have chosen to write a poem about the Sierras. Point out to students that Siebert describes changes that have taken place in the mountains over millions of years. Ask students to skim the poem to find some of these changes. Then ask a volunteer to read the last stanza of the poem. Discuss with students the meaning of Siebert's warning that the mountains depend on how people care for them.

Have students write a letter to Diane Siebert describing how people can take care of the mountains. After students have completed their letters, have volunteers read theirs to the class. Encourage students to mail their letters to Siebert.

# ROLL ON, COLUMBIA
**by Woody Guthrie**
**Pages 142–143** 📼

*Use with Chapter 11, Lesson 3*

## Objectives

❏ *Recognize how Woody Guthrie's song conveys the beauty and importance of the Columbia River.*

❏ *Identify the route of the Columbia River.*

## Tracing a Route

After students have read the lyrics to the song, play it for them on the cassette. Students may enjoy singing along with the cassette. Tell students that they are listening to Woody Guthrie sing his own song. Discuss with students why Woody Guthrie wrote a song about the Columbia River and electric power. Point out to students that the hydroelectric power from the Columbia River brought electricity to millions of people.

Have students trace the route of the Columbia River on a map of North America. Ask questions such as: *The Columbia River forms part of the border of which two states?* (Oregon and Washington) *Through what mountain ranges does it flow?* (Coast Ranges, Cascade Range) *In what other country does the Columbia River flow?* (Canada)

# A WALK THROUGH MY RAIN FOREST

**By Isaac Olaleye**
**Page 144** 📼

*Use with Chapter 11, Global Connections*

## Objectives

❑ *Describe a Nigerian rain forest.*
❑ *Compare the Nigerian rain forest to other forests in the world.*
❑ *Write a comparison of forests in two different regions.*

### Writing a Comparison

After students have read the poem, play the recording for them on the cassette. Then ask several volunteers to read the poem aloud. Ask students to name some of the "unexpected wonders" Isaac Olaleye sees in the rain forest. (for example, a blizzard of butterflies, an outpouring of mockingbirds, resurrection lily, zigzag begonia) Have students discuss how the Nigerian rain forest compares with an Amazon rain forest in Brazil or with a Western forest in America. Similarities and differences can be listed on the chalkboard.

After the discussion of rain forest comparisons, have students team up in pairs. Guide students in finding more information about forests around the world. Each student can research a particular forest. Then have students write a comparison of two rain forests. Paired students can give feedback and edit each other's descriptions. Students may wish to illustrate their comparisons for a class display of rain forest essays.

# WHEN THE WIND BLOWS HARD

**by Denise Gosliner Orenstein**
**Pages 145–148**

*Use with Chapter 11, Legacy, and Chapter 12, Lesson 1*

## Objectives

❑ *Recognize some characteristics of Tlingit culture.*
❑ *Identify symbols on a totem pole.*
❑ *Write a biography of Vesta's grandfather.*

### Writing a Biography

After students have read the story, discuss it with them. Ask volunteers to describe what Shawn learned about woodcarving during her visit with Vesta's grandfather. (Carving is an art that is treated as something alive and respected.) Then ask volunteers to describe what Shawn learned about the Tlingit's totem poles. (A symbolic animal is on top; people paint the poles while the poles are lying on the ground.) Ask volunteers to describe the totem pole animals. (The fox, the crab, and the mosquito represent a child, a thief, and teaching, respectively.) Ask students to describe what Shawn learned about the Tlingit and gifts. (The Tlingit never refuse a gift but accept it with open arms.)

Have students write a short biography of Vesta's grandfather based on the information they have read in the selection. Suggest that students illustrate their biographies with drawings of Vesta's grandfather's carving or totem pole. Have volunteers read their biographies to the rest of the class.

# BY THE GREAT HORN SPOON!
**by Sid Fleischman**
**Pages 149–151**

*Use with Chapter 12, Lesson 2*

## Objectives

❑ *Recognize why Jack and Praiseworthy went to California during the mid-1800s.*

❑ *Recognize some of the hardships of mining camps during the Gold Rush.*

❑ *Perform a Readers Theater of By the Great Horn Spoon!*

## Using Readers Theater

After students have read the selection, discuss it with them. Ask students to describe how Jack and Praiseworthy were typical of other Forty-Niners. (They went to California to get rich quick and then leave.) Then ask students what Jack and Praiseworthy had learned by the end of the story. (that getting rich quick was not going to be as easy as they hoped)

Have students perform *By the Great Horn Spoon!* as Readers Theater. Remind students that in a Readers Theater performance, the actors do not move around on a stage but remain seated and use only their voices as a means to act out the dialogue. The selection gives students an opportunity to read some interesting vocabulary. Choose students to take the parts of Jack, Praiseworthy, the waiter, the miner, and the narrator. Several students might take the parts of other miners in the camp. Encourage students to familiarize themselves with their lines before the performance.

# THE HEAVY PANTS OF MR. STRAUSS
**by June Swanson**
**Pages 152–153**

*Use with Chapter 12, Lesson 2*

## Objectives

❑ *Recognize why Levi Strauss invented blue jeans.*

❑ *Identify the advantages of Levi's as shown in the advertisement.*

❑ *Create an advertisement.*

## Creating an Advertisement

After students have read the essay, discuss it with them. Ask volunteers to explain the connection between the California Gold Rush and the invention of blue jeans. (The miners needed pants tough enough to stand up against rocks and the hard mining life.) Ask students: *What is the origin of the word* denim? (de Nimes) *What is the origin of the word* Levi's? (Levi Strauss)

Have students look at the advertisement that accompanies this essay. Point out the two horses pulling the Levi's in opposite directions. Ask volunteers to describe the meaning of the ad. (It emphasizes the strength and toughness of the fabric.) Then ask volunteers to describe in what way today's ads differ from the ad shown with the essay. (Today's ads focus on Levi's for leisure wear.) Point out to students that today the Levi's logo is widely recognized.

Have students draw an original advertisement for blue jeans. Suggest to students that they think about when and how they wear their blue jeans. Encourage them to draw a creative advertisement. Display students' completed advertisements on the bulletin board, titled "Blue Jeans Today."

# WAITING ON WYOMING

by Navidad O'Neill
Pages 154–161

Use with Chapter 12, Lesson 3

## Objectives

- ☐ *Recognize why the territory of Wyoming was important in the women's suffrage movement in 1869.*
- ☐ *List the reasons people were for and against women voting in Wyoming.*
- ☐ *Perform the play* Waiting on Wyoming.

### Performing a Play

After students have read the play, discuss it with them. Ask students why the territory of Wyoming is important in the history of the women's suffrage movement. (In 1869 Wyoming allowed women to vote in its elections—the first place in this country where women could do so.) Have students list the reasons people were for and against women voting. (For example, *for:* women should have same rights as men; *against:* women will become like men.) Have students brainstorm ideas on how they can perform the play; for example, who will play the characters, what costumes and props can be used, where the play will be set, and so on.

After the brainstorming session, divide the class into three groups: students who volunteer to be the student director, stage manager, and prop people; students who will play the characters from Wyoming; and students who will play the chorus of newspaper editors back East. List on the chalkboard the names of students playing the characters (stage managers can keep a record, too). With student directors and stage managers, work out the play's blocking and movement. Lay out a rehearsal schedule and decide on simple scenery (colorful signs) and costumes (for example, long skirts for girls) to show place and time. Form costume and prop committees. Make sure students know their lines before performing the play.

# HECTOR LIVES IN THE UNITED STATES NOW

by Joan Hewett
Pages 162–166

Use with Chapter 12, Lesson 4

## Objectives

- ☐ *Recognize some of the difficulties encountered by Hector Almaraz, an immigrant to the United States from Mexico.*
- ☐ *Identify some of the important events in Hector's life.*
- ☐ *Draw a storyboard with captions.*

### Drawing Storyboards with Captions

After students have read the selection, have them identify the problem that Hector faced when he started kindergarten. (He could not understand or speak English.) Have students suggest other problems that immigrants to the United States often face. (lack of familiarity with customs, loneliness, economic hardship, and so on) Then have students compare and contrast Hector's life in the United States with their own.

Have ten groups of students prepare storyboards from *Hector Lives in the United States Now* to plan a video. Ask each group of students to draw a scene that represents one of the following parts of the selection: 1. Hector's family; 2. Hector and his friends playing games; 3. Hector and his friends on the front stoop; 4. Hector and his brother at the kitchen table; 5. Hector in kindergarten; 6. Hector in fifth grade; 7. Philip, Nicky, Vanessa, Erick, Julie, Kyria, and Hector with their ancestors; 8. Hector working on a computer at the library; 9. Hector reading at home; 10. Hector and his family going to Mexico. Have students write captions for their storyboards. After students have completed the storyboards, make a display of them on a bulletin board.

# A MOUNTAIN VIEW
**by Rose Burgunder**
**Page 167**

---

*Use with Chapter 11, Lesson 1*

## Objectives

- ❑ *Recognize the natural beauty of the Sierra Nevada mountain range as described in "A Mountain View."*
- ❑ *Identify how Rose Burgunder describes the view during a Western sunset.*
- ❑ *Create a poster of the Sierra Nevada during sunset or sunrise.*

## Creating a Poster

After students have read the poem, play it for them on the cassette. After listening to it, volunteers might enjoy reading the poem aloud. Have students point out images in the poem that describe the mountain range's natural beauty. (snow on the soft blue range) Ask students why they think the poet doesn't want the mountains to change. (It is beautiful the way it is.)

Divide the class into three groups. Instruct each group to draw a poster of the Sierra Nevada mountain range at a different time: during sunset; during sunrise; at another time, for example, at midday or evening. Before designing the poster, students in the group can discuss the effect of the changing light on the mountains. Students can print the poem "A Mountain View" on their poster or write new versions of the poem to account for the time of day. Display posters and poems on a bulletin board in the shape of a mountain range.